The 30-Second Encyclopedia of Learning and Performance

A Trainer's Guide to Theory, Terminology, and Practice

DAVID H. MILES, Ph.D.

AMACOM

American Management Association

New York • Atlanta • Brussels • Buenos Aires • Chicago • London • Mexico City
San Francisco • Shanghai • Tokyo • Toronto • Washington, D.C.

Special discounts on bulk quantities of AMACOM books are available to corporations, professional associations, and other organizations. For details, contact Special Sales Department, AMACOM, a division of American Management Association, 1601 Broadway, New York, NY 10019.
Tel.: 212-903-8316.   Fax: 212-903-8083.
Web site: www.amacombooks.org

This publication is designed to provide accurate and authoritative information in regard to the subject matter covered. It is sold with the understanding that the publisher is not engaged in rendering legal, accounting, or other professional service. If legal advice or other expert assistance is required, the services of a competent professional person should be sought.

Library of Congress Cataloging-in-Publication Data

Miles, David H.
    The 30-second encyclopedia of learning and performance : a trainer's guide to theory, terminology, and practice / David H. Miles.
        p.   cm.
    Includes bibliographical references and index.
    ISBN 0-8144-7178-1 (pbk.)
    1. Training—Handbooks, manuals, etc.   I. Title.

LB1027.47.M54 2003
370.11'3—dc21   2003002551

Printing number

10   9   8   7   6   5   4   3   2   1

Contents

Acknowledgments

I would like to acknowledge the efforts of the following individuals who knowingly or unknowingly aided and abetted this book. These include Roger Chevalier, Robert and Harriet Gagne, M. David Merrill, Mark Morrow, William Rothwell, Geary Rummler, and Ron Zemke. I am also indebted to the many clients and colleagues with whom I have worked over the years, which include AT&T, The Bank of America, Docent, Panasonic Broadcast Systems, Toyota, Wilson Learning, and Xerox. I would also like to express my gratitude to two editorial magicians— Jacquie Flynn, senior acquisitions editor at AMACOM, and Niels Buessem of Andover Publishing Services. And my final thanks go to my wife Lori Gordon Miles, who marshaled her own considerable writing talents as well as her jargon-detector to help keep this project on track.

Introduction

There's nothing so practical as a good theory.
—Kurt Lewin, 1940

I'll excite their minds with the desire to know.
—Milton, *Paradise Lost*, 1667

Why This Book: First Principles and a Common Language

"Every professional language," George Bernard Shaw once quipped, "is a conspiracy against the laity." The field of learning and performance is no different. Even within this relatively small discipline there are subdisciplines, each one spouting its own code jargon and making it difficult for beginners and even professionals to communicate readily with one another, let alone with clients. The International Society for Performance Improvement (ISPI), for instance, speaks of "human performance technology"; the American Society for Training & Development (ASTD) speaks of "performance improvement"; and organizational developers speak of "interventions and change management initiatives." All three speak of "knowledge management"—and yet mean something different by it in each case.

I compiled this book because of the need for a common language in the learning and performance field. When I first entered the field some twenty years ago (when it was called training and development), most of the information to be found was in unreadable five-pound textbooks and 800-page handbooks. Moreover, the field seemed less a discipline than a series of fads, fashions, and flavors of the month. By now, the field has existed for over a century since its beginnings, and it seemed to me as good a time as any for clearing the ground for a foundational discipline—for rethinking and reformulating first principles. With clearer definitions and philosophical distinctions, the field will be able to continue to thrive, and to carry even more impact than it has in the past.

How to Use This Book: The 30-Second Access

The book is designed as a multilevel database: You can jump in at any level and retrieve the information required—from a one-sentence definition of "systems," for instance, to an extensive range of research on the art of designing systems. The book aims to provide you with the information you need at the moment you need it—be it Information Lite or Deep Data. Here is the way three different user levels would utilize the book:

Beginners:

■ Have you suddenly been catapulted into a training department without a Ph.D. from Harvard? Don't know what they're talking about in meetings? Read this little book when you're back at your desk. It will ramp you up quickly and point you in the right direction.

■ For a brief systematic introduction, read Part One, from beginning to end, to gain an overview of the learning and performance improvement process, from analysis through solution-design to implementation and evaluation.

Intermediates:

■ Using the table of contents and the index, you can locate any subject ("learning object") and read the initial definition within thirty seconds. Spend a couple of minutes reading the rest of the entry or certain cross-references—then go have lunch or go to your next meeting (or, if you have the afternoon off, go read one of the five-pound textbooks I have referenced in the Fastpaths sections).

Advanced Practitioners:

■ A practicing expert and know everything? Kick back on your next lunch break and read the section on "Dante: Curriculum as Memory Theatre" in Part Three, and let your brain rock and roll on sun storms of association toward a new award-winning learning and performance initiative!

The Fastpaths as Pointers to Expert Texts

Throughout the book there are chronological listings of key events in the development of the different theories and concepts, called Fastpaths.

These Fastpath sections, which provide a sense of the historical development of each concept, are of particular interest to advanced practitioners and researchers. Practitioners looking for only practical steps can skip these listings.

Some Definitions

Learning vs. Performance

A word about how the terms "learning" and "performance" are used in this book. "Learning" refers to the acquisition of skills, knowledge, and attitude—through instruction, self-study, or coaching. "Performance" refers to the deployment of these newly acquired skills in the workplace, and the concrete results of these efforts. The two words form a sequence, as follows:

- *Learning:* designates the *acquisition* of new skills, knowledge, or attitudes
- *Performance:* designates the *results* produced by putting this learning into practice on the job

Training vs. Learning

The word "training," which I also use liberally in this book, is an older designation. The trainer-centric world is now shifting, in the twenty-first century, to a learner-centric one. It's all a matter of perspective. Because not all organizations make this distinction, however, I use learning and training interchangeably in this book.

Training vs. Education

Education, much like training, refers to the acquisition of knowledge, skills, and attitudes. But—to oversimplify the point—education is to training as theory is to practice. To cite the old saw: Sex education is not the same thing as sex training. The distinction actually goes back to the industrial age of the 1800s, when education (traditionally associated with morality and the religious tradition) was viewed in opposition to training, which was associated with the rise of the new vocational schools. Education is the broader, more generalized term, whereas training is specific to real-world jobs.

Core Concepts vs. General Concepts

The core concepts and general concepts discussed in Parts One and Two of this book were originally one long alphabetical list. For reasons of speedier access, however, I decided to move four core concepts and processes—needs assessment, instructional systems design, evaluation, and systems—to the front, as Part One. These are the top four concepts that most practitioners have to deal with on a daily basis, so it's handy to have them in a separate section. Taken together, however, Parts One and Two can actually be viewed as a single list of concepts, processes, and terms. Frequent cross-references throughout the book help facilitate jumps to relevant and related information.

A Note to Researchers

To conserve space, I have confined most of the citations to *books rather than to articles.* For book citations, I have given *the original date of publication,* in order to highlight the continuity and historical development of the ideas involved. In many cases, this helps one grasp their wider meaning. For those interested in locating the most recent edition of any particular work, Amazon.com is the fastest source.

For those interested in locating the *publisher and place* of a book listed, any online state university library can readily provide that information, such as California's www.melvyl.ucop.edu or Ohio's www.ohio link.edu. The latter also provides OCLC numbers (online computer library center) for ordering interlibrary loans. Many of the standard works on learning psychology are listed at http://psychclassics.yorku.ca.

Information Web Sites of Associations

Additional industry information can be found on Web sites of the following professional associations:

American Management Association (AMA): www.amanet.org
American Society for Training & Development (ASTD): www.astd.org
International Society for Performance Improvement (ISPI): www.ispi.org
Organization Development Network: www.odnetwork.org

Suggestions for the Next Edition:
E-Mail Address

Please send suggestions or corrections for the next edition of this work to:

Ldmiles@pacbell.net

Thank you!

Dive in anywhere and enjoy yourself.
This book is for beginners and advanced practitioners alike!

I. CORE CONCEPTS AND PROCESS MODELS

Proceed by process . . .
—Shakespeare, *Coriolanus,* 1608

The Needs Assessment

Teach them to observe all things.
    —Matthew 28:20

Happy the man who has learned the causes of things.
    —Virgil, 20 B.C.

Definition and Components

A needs assessment is *a systematic study or survey of an organization for the purpose of making recommendations,* and is often employed in performance consulting to get to the cause of a performance problem. Thus typically, a needs assessment consists of a survey plus recommendations. Although the term "needs assessment" itself can refer to bald-faced promotions ("We'll do a needs assessment for your department and show you how our solution will meet all your performance needs") or simple order-taking questionnaires ("What off-the-shelf courses are needed to train our employees on the new system?"), we shall use it here to refer to the first step in performance consulting ("How can we make our call center more effective?"). A needs assessment generally consists of three parts: a survey, an analysis, and a recommendation.

Because needs assessments comprise the initial phase of many problem-solving processes, they can be part of any of the following process models: the analysis phase of the ADDIE instructional design model, the diagnosis phase of the human performance technology (HPT) model, the diagnosis phase of the organizational development (OD) model, and the diagnosis phase of general performance consulting. Thus, needs assessments go under a variety of names, including needs analysis, front-end analysis, planning needs analysis, strategic needs analysis, and training needs analysis. All refer, however, to the same thing.

Phases

The three phases of carrying out a needs assessment are design, deployment, and reporting, as follows:

I. DESIGN: The Five Methods of Data Gathering

It is a capital mistake to theorize before one has data.
                    —Sherlock Holmes, *A Scandal in Bohemia*, 1891

I must begin, not with hypotheses, but with specific instances.
                    —Paul Klee, 1931

The five general methods for gathering data about a business, a specific need, or a performance problem, are:

1. *Direct Observation.* This consists of simply looking about with a trained and focused eye—the "environmental scan" that "believes what it sees, not what it hears." Often overlooked, direct observation is often a valuable method for gathering information for a needs analysis. Without a cool-eyed look at "the facts," prescribing solutions will accomplish little. A good needs assessor is also a good private eye.

2. *Existing Documents.* Also called *extant data* gathering. This could include anything from mission statements and organization charts to business objectives, annual plans, production numbers, and job descriptions.

3. *Group Interviews.* Small-group interviews, which may officially be called "focus groups," are often employed to get reactions to a specific proposed initiative.

4. *Individual Interviews.* These can be either face-to-face interviews, or structured interviews on the phone (using a questionnaire). One interview tip: Design these oral interviews to lead with *open* questions (such as, "Tell me about the situation") and to end with *closed* questions ("Do you like this feature of the new software or not?"). The initial open questions will yield more qualitative information, and the closed questions will yield more quantitative data. Both are useful in a needs assessment.

5. *Written Surveys.* These can be administered via e-mail, Web, or hard-copy, and typically ask both open questions (including "critical incidents") and closed questions (yes/no, multiple-choice, or the 1–5 Likert scale). They include the following:

- What are your business goals?
- What are your challenges?
- What are the opportunities?
- What are the barriers?
- What are the key skills and knowledge required?

TIP Short and Simple

Keep needs assessments short and simple. Generally you don't have a Big Five consulting firm at your disposal to implement them. A small sample population representing a cross-section of your audience, plus a one-page questionnaire with less than a dozen questions, should suffice. Large-scale needs assessments can consume enormous amounts of time and money and, unless held in check, can produce such a flood of data that only *analysis paralysis* can result. Keep needs assessments focused and confined.

II. DEPLOYMENT: Interviews and the Four Respondent Groups

My job is to ask the right questions. I ask very simple questions. Managers and executives can't answer them.

—Peter Drucker, 2001

The information sources (interviewees) in a needs assessment might include the following:

1. Target audience:
   - Exemplary performers (star performers, masters)
   - Average performers (to determine the accomplishments differential, gap, or performance improvement opportunity involved)
2. Managers of target group
3. Direct reports of target group
4. Other stakeholders, sponsors, or corporate champions

III. SUMMARY: Reports and Recommendations

The world is full of obvious things that nobody observes.
—Sherlock Holmes, *The Hound of the Baskervilles*, 1902

A needs assessment generally culminates in a summary of the survey results, an identification of the problem, and general recommendations for addressing the situation. A final report might recommend coaching sessions, a new class, smoother processes between departments, or a new compensation plan. The typical components of a report are:

- Executive summary
- Findings
   Compilation and analysis of survey data
   Identification of themes from the qualitative responses (from open questions)
   Tabulation of quantitative responses (from closed questions)
- Strategy with recommendations and a plan
- Appendix: Questionnaire, respondents, method used

Deep Needs Assessments: Task Analysis

In order to complete the diagnosis of some business processes, it is sometimes necessary to drill down to the task analysis level, the granular level at which processes are broken up into their smallest constituent parts and examined. This is not for the faint of heart, for the process of reduction or "decomposition" of processes into tasks can be arduous and complex. Luckily, however, there exist two superb texts on the procedure: Ron Zemke's classic book, *Figuring Things Out: A Trainer's Guide to Needs and Task Analysis* (1982), and Jeroen van Merrienboer's study, *Training Complex Cognitive Skills* (1997). Zemke's is accessible to beginners; Merrienboer's is for professionals.

FASTPATHS

1970   Joe Harless: *An Ounce of Analysis Is Worth a Pound of Objectives.* Harless, reaching for an assembly-line term from the manufacturing industry, coins the term *"front-end" analysis,* which means the same thing as a needs assessment. Harless's main contribution was to emphasize that analysis of needs should come *before* everything else—including the writing of objectives.

1970   Robert Mager and P. Pipe: *Analyzing Performance Problems or You Really Oughta Wanna*. A classic in the field of performance analysis, updated many times since.

1978   Tom Gilbert: *Human Competence: Engineering Worthy Performance*. For more on this work, see the section on Human Performance Technology (HPT).

1979   Roger Kaufman and F. English: *Needs Assessment*.

1982   Ron Zemke and T. Kramlinger: *Figuring Things Out: A Trainer's Guide to Needs and Task Analysis*. One of the best books ever written on needs assessments and task analyses. Key book for any performance consultant or instructional designer.

1987   Allison Rossett: *Training Needs Assessment*. An exceptionally clear exposition of the topic.

1995   John Noonan: *Elevators: How to Move Training Up from the Basement*. Contains a chapter that serves as an excellent introduction to needs assessments for beginners.

1997   Jeroen van Merrienboer: *Training Complex Cognitive Skills*. The chapters on decomposition (breaking down) of cognitive content are relevant—if task analysis is part of the needs assessment. A book for professionals.

1998   Allison Rossett*: First Things Fast: A Handbook for Performance Analysis*. A follow-on to her 1987 work.

1999   David Jonassen, et al.: *Task Analysis Methods for Instructional Design*.

TIP   Four Tips on Needs Assessments

Tip 1: *Use the journalist's five Ws.* The performance consultant asks the same questions that the investigative journalist does: "who, what, where, when, why." Generally, the more specific the question, the more useful the data.

Tip 2: *Use hunches wisely.* No business unit wants to tell you everything that's wrong with it, so the task of the needs assessor is partially one of deduction and inference. In needs analysis one gets to perform detection work, uncovering information through informal conversations, observations, and intuitions. Needs assessments can confirm a hunch about what's going on in a company (although one obviously needs to avoid purely "self-fulfilling prophecies").

Tip 3: *Be a sleuth, not a statistician.* Needs assessments generally call for good common sense plus some sense of sleuthing rather than the skills of a scientist or an advanced statistician. Don't make the task more difficult than it is.

Tip 4: *View a business from four angles.* There are four angles to any business, and one way to structure a needs assessment is around these four perspectives:

1. People
2. Processes
3. Strategy
4. Technology

Instructional Systems Design

Instructional Systems History: From Oral Performance Coaching to Written Design

We learn best when we learn through a systems approach.
—Comenius, *The Great Didactic*, 1650

The earliest instruction in recorded history was not training in our modern sense, but what we would today call performance support or coached performance improvement. The ancient Greeks, focused on oral coaching, delivered hands-on apprenticeships coupled with extensive mentoring. The word "mentor," in fact, derives from a figure in Homer's *Odyssey* who acted as a life-long learning guide to the hero's son. Similarly, the early Romans also insisted on hands-on apprenticeships; nothing was allowed to be taught that couldn't be instructed while the student was actually at work. Learning was on-the-job performance support, or it was nothing.

During the Middle Ages, the guilds (medieval trade unions) organized their training into performance-centered systems in which learners developed skills through competency-based exams and were certified as either *apprentice, journeyman*, or *master* performer. Always there was coaching and mentoring alongside the practical daily experience of the apprenticeship. One learned, quite simply, by doing.

As the age of agriculture slowly gave way, in the 1700s and 1800s, to the industrial age, a gradual shift occurred, and there started to appear the first vocational institutes in the form of factory and correspondence schools, our first distance learning institutions. The precursor of written instructional design was the teacher's "lesson plan"—in which were recorded the objectives for the curriculum together with the learning solution. The learning solution—which typically combined book readings, lectures, written exercises, oral discussions, and tests—was, in effect, the original "blended" solution.

Instructional design (ID) did not become a full-fledged profession, however, until World War II, when it was literally born under gunfire. Instructional designers were suddenly needed to create training courses for the complex operations of highly technical military assault weapons—air force planes, navy submarines, and computerized anti-aircraft guns. They also invented the army training film and introduced the new discipline of "human factors" (to complement the "machine factors"), which was such an essential part of the new high-performing defense systems. Not surprisingly, the American Society for Training and Development (ASTD) was also launched at the height of World War II, in 1943. (See also Human Factors and Ergonomics.)

During these early pioneer days of instructional design, behaviorist systems reigned supreme, and for good reason. Designers were creating courses that primarily taught an intricate series of physical tasks requiring split-second timing, and a behaviorist model was ideal for this. The Army Air Corps needed training designers who, in the words of Robert Gagne, "could transform farm boys into airplane mechanics in thirty days instead of two years." The key to success (a principle still valid today) was the breaking down or "decomposition" of training into small behavioral units or steps, followed by the proper sequencing of these steps. Taught and applied appropriately, the technique was enormously successful.

From its inception during the War, instructional design was also automatically "systems" design ("big picture" design incorporating intricate, interlocking parts and procedures rather than "piecemeal" design), for at the heart of the war effort was the need to train on how to operate complex, computerized weapon systems (rather than mechanical weapon systems).

In the 1950s, following World War II, B. F. Skinner and the behaviorists carried this systems campaign into civilian territory, with their promotion of the new technology of the automated teaching machine (which primarily taught sequential procedures), and the "programmed instruction" (PI) movement was born. This movement announced that small-step instructions, with interactive branching possibilities, would bring radical cost reductions to training. To some extent it did, and on the strength of this, behaviorist programmed instruction, with its detailed sequences of small steps, took hold as a major movement during the

1960s. Its strategy of intricate, branching interactivity led in turn to the computer-based training (CBT) movement of the 1970s. Modern computers could support the rigorous branching demands much better than could the mechanical teaching machine.

By the mid-1970s, instructional design had matured to the point where, in a series of white papers from both civilian and military sectors, it announced a systems model of its own called "ADDIE." ADDIE (which, although unnamed, had actually been in widespread use since the 1950s) stood for the formal instructional design process of "Analysis, Design, Development, Implementation, and Evaluation," which went into the creation of classroom training. We shall have more to say about this in a moment.

Instructional Systems Roles: Information Architect, Knowledge Designer, and User Advocate

Instructional systems designers are the Grand Architects of Content. They are the blueprint designers, outliners, and sometimes the actual writers of the content. Generally speaking, however, they work in tandem with writers and with content experts (SMEs, or subject matter experts). If a user manual or a VCR guide is unreadable, for example, it probably means that no instructional designer was hired to guide the technical writer and the engineer involved.

Instructional designers generally research, organize, and outline courses within a framework including considerations of:

- Business objectives (reducing training expenses or enhancing revenue)
- End user context (real-world business situation)
- Learning objectives (knowledge, skills, and attitudes)
- Evaluation (the four levels)

The information for this process is gathered through informal conversations, reviews of existing documentation, and needs assessments. And finally, it is shaped into proper form—the three hallmarks of proper design being:

- Clearly organized content
  Chunking: dividing content into its proper constituent parts
  Sequencing: linking the chunks or components together into an organized whole
- Clear layout
  Appropriate subheads, plenty of white space, and easy-on-the-eyes composition of information on the page (see Information Mapping)
- Clear writing
  Structured writing in brief, concise paragraphs

To sum up, instructional designers perform a wide variety of functions, including those of information architect, knowledge designer, and user advocate. With the maturation of the Web as a delivery medium, and with the rising need for performance support systems (online help), content is shifting more and more from entire "courses" to small "knowledge chunks" (stand-alone paragraphs), and thus the instructional designer needs to function as a content "assembler" or "compiler" as well as an outliner. Knowledge management systems (databases featuring bite-sized chunks of learning) require instructional designers to work in tandem with database designers. And throughout these processes, the designer must also function as a "user advocate," defending the end user's right to an effective learning experience in a real-world context. Thus the designer must validate, through interim and final product tests, that the course or system will deliver what it promises.

Finally, instructional design is the art of the invisible. Instructional designers, like the best film editors and interface designers, function as "vanishing mediators." For in the final analysis the end-user should perceive only the course content, and not its "design." The hallmark of good design is total transparency.

FASTPATHS

1940–1945   World War II. The field of instructional design is born, being firmly rooted in the behaviorist psychology of Thorndike, Watson, and Skinner (see Behaviorism).

1959   Robert M. Gagne (1916–2002) coauthors, with Edward Fleishman, the behaviorist textbook, *Psychology and Human Performance*.

1962	Robert Gagne edits the anthology *Psychological Principles in System Development,* which includes a chapter by Meredith Crawford on systems thinking in instructional design, with a prototype for the ADDIE model developed in the 1950s by the U.S. army.
1965	Robert Gagne: *The Conditions of Learning.* A classic in the history of instructional design, the term "conditions" in the title referring indirectly to its roots in the theory of behaviorist conditioning. Gagne takes up Bloom's classic triad of knowledge, skills, and attitudes from 1956 and divides the "knowledge" domain further—into intellectual, verbal, and cognitive. Although Merrienboer's 1997 book (see below) is perhaps the more useful text today, Gagne, a psychology Ph.D. from Brown University whose skills were honed in military training during World War II, was a pioneer in the field, one of the prime movers behind early instructional design.
1974	Robert Gagne and Leslie Briggs of Florida State University publish *The Principles of Instructional Design*, a systematic look at instructional design that still remains a mainstay text today.
1975	The official birth of instructional systems development (ISD), with its five steps of analysis, design, development, implementation, and evaluation (ADDIE). Actually, the model had been in development and use since the 1950s in both military and civilian training. ISD fast becomes the standard model for instructional design.
1978	Walter Dick and Lou Carey: *The Systematic Design of Instruction.* One of the founding texts for a systems view of instructional design. Latest edition still useful.
1983	Charles Reigeluth (ed.): *Instructional Design Theories and Models: An Overview.* First volume in a series of anthologies useful for professionals.
1985	Jerrold Kemp: *The Instructional Design Process.* Classic text on instructional design. Latest edition still useful.
1987	Charles Reigeluth (ed.): *Instructional Theories in Action.* Second volume in a series of anthologies useful for professionals.
1989	Ruth Clark: *Developing Technical Training: A Structured Approach.* Good summary of how to design and develop computer-based training (CBT), including structured writing and clear information design.
1992	William Rothwell and H. Kazanas: *Mastering the Instructional Design Process: A Systematic Approach.* Excellent summary of instructional design theories and processes. One of the best textbooks available.

1992   Cynthia Leshin (ed.): *Instructional Design: Strategies and Tactics*.

1993   Patricia Smith and T. Ragan: *Instructional Design*.

1994   M. David Merrill: *Instructional Design Theory*. Merrill is a leader in the field of instructional design. His book contains, among other insights, a useful taxonomy of content (facts vs. concepts vs. processes) as well as a differentiation of performance outcomes (cognitive recall vs. on-the-job behavior).

1995   John Noonan: *Elevators: How to Move Training Up from the Basement*. Despite the clunky title, a well-written introduction to instructional design for beginners, including needs assessments, analysis and planning, design and development, and with a creative suggestion for extrapolating Level 4 ROI from Level 1 interview data. This often overlooked title is recommended as an introduction.

1996   Tom Boyle: *Design for Multimedia Learning*.

1996   Angus Reynolds and Thomas Iwinski: *Multimedia Training: Developing Technology-Based Systems*.

1996   Vincent Miller: "The History of Training," *The ASTD Training and Development Handbook*.

1997   Jeroen J. G. van Merrienboer: *Training Complex Cognitive Skills*. A textbook for advanced professionals, extremely clear on the "decomposition" of cognitive skills into steps.

1998   Michael Milano: *Designing Powerful Training*.

1999   Charles Reigeluth (ed.): *Instructional-Design Theories and Models: A New Paradigm of Instructional Theory*. Third volume in a series of anthologies useful for professionals.

2000   George Piskurich: *Rapid Instructional Design*. Stands out among a multitude of systems-oriented textbooks.

See also
Behaviorism
Cognitivism

Instructional Design Models

There is no end to the making of instructional design models. There are new ones being invented literally every day. Therefore, it should be stated here unequivocally that there is no one best or correct model. Rigid adherence to any particular methodology would be self-defeating. Models are rules of thumb (heuristics), guidelines to help one through a process, and as such they should be customized to the business situation at hand and taken in that spirit.

There are two types of models for the design and development of instructional systems, the first being the traditional ADDIE model developed for classroom design, the second being an expanded version, tailored specifically for blended or e-learning environments. I developed the latter model, Dimension 7, myself and have used it successfully on implementations for several years now. Because the Web is a dynamic environment, it requires a substantially different model from the classroom.

THE CLASSROOM MODEL: ADDIE

Even though ADDIE has been in use for over a half century, it still provides a solid and useful model for building classroom training. It consists of the following five straightforward steps. (These will be defined in more detail in the subsequent section on Dimension 7.)

1. Analysis
2. Design
3. Development
4. Implementation
5. Evaluation

THE WEB MODEL: Dimension 7

The Web launched the world's first truly dynamic learning environment, enabling continuous learning systems in which courses could be centrally upgraded on the fly. Building courseware for the Web became not a one-time event, but a continuous process. Thus the structure of the Dimension 7 model for the Web is essentially circular—one long, continuous loop (see Figure 1). One can, as with ADDIE, expand, telescope, or modify any one of the seven steps involved.

1. Discovery Phase (Analysis)

The discovery phase of instructional design equates to the analysis phase of ADDIE. It consists of evidence-gathering: posing questions, running

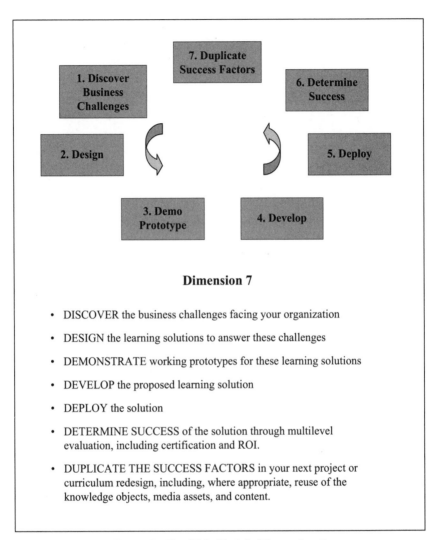

Dimension 7

- DISCOVER the business challenges facing your organization
- DESIGN the learning solutions to answer these challenges
- DEMONSTRATE working prototypes for these learning solutions
- DEVELOP the proposed learning solution
- DEPLOY the solution
- DETERMINE SUCCESS of the solution through multilevel evaluation, including certification and ROI.
- DUPLICATE THE SUCCESS FACTORS in your next project or curriculum redesign, including, where appropriate, reuse of the knowledge objects, media assets, and content.

**Figure 1. The Web Model: Dimension 7:
Designing and Developing a Course or Curriculum.**

needs analyses, and requesting documents. The instructional designer typically conducts this phase of the project, doing the interviews and carrying out the research and analysis. Typical issues addressed in this phase are:

- ■ Current business problem
- ■ Future business goal

- Gap between current and desired performance
- Profile of target audience
- Analysis of job being performed
- Identification of the training solution
- Identification of delivery medium (classroom, Web, etc.) and infrastructure considerations
- Identification of team members and resources
- Budget and timeline constraints
- Measurement of success for the training

The product of the discovery phase is an analysis report or "scoping" document, a brief summary document that sizes the problem and integrates the findings. It is generally submitted to management for financial approval of the project. This scoping document also identifies any potential political hurdles or technological constraints. Because it sets the stage and expectations for the entire project, this document must be attended to with care and precision.

See also
Needs Assessment
Performance Improvement and Performance Consulting

2. Design Phase

The design phase consists of outlining the course and includes two subphases: an initial broad outline called the "high-level" design, and a more specific one called the "detailed" design document. Again, this phase is carried out by the instructional designer or writer on the project, in conjunction with the rest of the team, which might include the subject matter expert, a representative from the target audience, and a project manager.

■ *High-Level Design.* Sometimes called macro-design, this phase produces an outline that gives a bird's eye view of the course, including business goals, learning objectives, target audience, chief topics, types of tests or certifications involved, timeline, and budget. This outline adds more detail now that the budget and timeline have been approved, and fine-tunes the scoping document accordingly.

■ *Detailed-Level Design.* Sometimes called micro-design, this phase produces an outline that adds detailed content to the previous outline's skeletal structure. Topics are broken out into subtopics (units, lessons, modules), learning objectives into sub-objectives (knowledge, skills, and attitudes), and tests into subtests. All components are then properly sequenced together and related to the learning objectives or outcomes. This dual process of decomposition and re-linking is referred to as the "chunking and sequencing" of the material.

Top Down and Bottom Up: Instructional Design as Database Design

Content designing a course is very similar to database design, for both jobs demand that the designer be an information architect. Experienced instructional designers, for instance, much like database designers, often employ a dual design strategy: they work simultaneously "top down" from the overall course outline (broad generalities) and "bottom up" from the individual user's point of view (concrete specifics). In instructional design circles this is sometimes called "reverse" design—because one is simultaneously designing from the detailed level view of the end-user as well as from the high-level view of the major course components. In this way one doesn't lose sight of the big picture OR the little one.

3. Demo Phase (Prototyping)

This phase, sometimes called rapid or iterative (repeated) prototyping, is more frequently used for software projects than for classrooms. It test-drives the detailed designs of the previous stage by building working prototypes. Because of the high expense of developing software, this step amounts to a cost-containment strategy.

4. Development Phase

The development phase consists of writing the course if it is classroom training, or of scripting, graphic-designing, and programming if it is a Web course. Because of the sizable differences at this stage depending upon the particular medium being employed (hardcopy, audio, video, etc.), we will use generic terms to designate the subphases of this stage:

■ *Alpha Version*: First draft
■ *Beta Version*: Second draft

- *Testing*: Quality assurance testing, validation of the course and any accompanying materials
- *Pilot*: Pilot-testing the course; in the case of classrooms, this can include train-the-trainer sessions
- *Final*: Final revision and sign-off

A word about team involvement during this phase. Classroom courses are developed by a professional writer, who is sometimes the same person as the instructional designer. In the case of Web courses, development is carried out by a team consisting of a writer, an HTML programmer, a graphics designer, and a database programmer. In the case of video, the team would consist of a writer, production crew (shooting), and post-production staff (editing).

5. Deployment Phase (Implementation)

This phase, consisting of duplication and distribution (classroom) or installing and configuring (Web), designates the launch or deployment of the course—to classrooms, Webscreens, or video monitors. If software-based, this phase also includes putting into place all maintenance, systems administration, content monitoring, and tech support.

6. Determination Phase (Evaluation)

This phase evaluates the course. Despite its placement here as a single step, this process is actually continuous, weaving in and out of the project during Phases 3 to 5 and during the subsequent 7th phase. As we point out elsewhere, this phase actually consists of four separate levels or subphases of evaluation, namely:

Level 1: Evaluating the course (how to improve the course)
Level 2: Evaluating knowledge of what was taught (e.g., tests and certifications)
Level 3: Evaluating application of course to on-the-job (transfer to the real world)
Level 4: Evaluating financial impact of course on the business (ROI and bottom-line profit)

7. Duplication Phase (Applying What Was Learned to Future Courses and Updates)

The duplication phase applies what you learned on this project to future projects, duplicating lessons learned to other courses in the curriculum. This phase is added to the static ADDIE model because of the dynamic nature of the Web curriculum, the ease with which content can be centrally updated and redeployed virtually overnight. This final Phase 7 then flows back into Phase 1 again—"discovery" for the next update. The Web model thus constitutes one long feedback-and-feedforward loop.

See also
Lessons Learned

Objectives: Knowledge, Skills, and Attitude

When it comes to objectives, Robert Mager's definition is still the best:

> An objective is the description of a performance you want learners to be able to exhibit, before you consider them competent.

Objectives, Mager adds, describe the *results* of instruction, not the instruction itself (*Preparing Instructional Objectives*, 1962). Furthermore, objectives can be of two types: *terminal* objectives, which refer to expected results at the end of the course, and *enabling* objectives, which are interim or subobjectives along the way.

Objectives Describe Outcomes, Not Processes

Strictly speaking, so-called behavioral or performance objectives are misnomers, for *behavior* and *performance* are process-words, and they do not describe the results. In business training, however, we are interested in results—and performance and behavior are only the means to an end. We should never lose sight of the fact that it is the *outcome* of a performance or a behavior that counts, not the performance or behavior itself.

The Three Components of an Objective

There are three components to a learning objective:

1. *A Performance*: what the employee will be doing, saying, or accomplishing
2. *Specific Conditions:* under what work circumstances and using what support tools does the task happen
3. *A Criterion:* a standard or required level of proficiency, how one will recognize success

Example of an Objective

Here is an example of a performance objective for the following task (skill):

> The learner will be able to draw a pistol, fire, and hit the behaviorist professor's trigger hand (disabling him) from a distance of thirty feet, at least four out of six times.

1. Performance: Draw a pistol, fire, and hit the behaviorist professor's trigger hand

2. Conditions: From a distance of thirty feet

3. Criterion: At least four out of six times

Knowledge, Skills, and Attitude

The types of objectives were clearly defined in the 1950s. At that time Benjamin Bloom, a behaviorist and founding father of competency-based learning, posited three "domains" of learning that have since become standard. They have been used as a baseline by practically every major practitioner in the field. Bloom described the three domains as follows:

■ KNOWLEDGE: The *cognitive* or thinking domain includes facts and information.

Example of Knowledge: "Score 90 percent on the certification exam."

■ SKILLS: The *psychomotor* or "doing" domain, which refers to physical on-the-job performance.

Example of a Skill: "Be able to word-process eighty words-a-minute, with less than one mistake per 100."

■ ATTITUDE: The *affective* or feeling domain.

Example of a Proper Attitude: "Obey the ten safety regulations while on the shop floor."

FASTPATHS

1949   Ralph Tyler, father of behavioral objectives, publishes *Basic Principles of Curriculum and Instruction.*

1954   Peter Drucker publishes article "Management by Objectives and Self-Control," stating that "each manager, from the top on down to the production foreman, needs clearly spelled-out objectives that clarify expected contributions to the company's goals."

1956   Benjamin Bloom, founder of behavioral objectives along with Tyler, publishes *Taxonomy of Educational Objectives: The Classification of Educational Goals.* In this classic text Bloom systematizes Tyler's objectives in a study of goal-directed learning and behavioral objectives, which also became a forerunner of today's "competencies." Bloom posits three broad categories of objectives: knowledge, skills, and attitude (cognitive, psychomotor, and affective domains). These domains still hold sway today. It should be pointed out that Bloom did not complete his taxonomy. After distinguishing six cognitive behaviors (knowledge,

---

The "A"-Word

Over the years, the third term in Bloom's triad of Knowledge, Skills, and Attitude has been referred to variously as Attributes (traits such as patience, judgment, and strength), Aptitudes (capabilities), and even Abilities (which confusingly would encompass both knowledge and skills as well). This terminological blurring is best sorted out and clarified by the individual practitioner.

Sidebar for Psychologists and Philosophers

Interestingly, Bloom's triad of performance domains actually mirrors classic psychology, in particular that of Plato.

Plato's Psychology		*Bloom's Psychology*
Organizational	*Individual*	*Individual*
Knowledge workers	Mind (head)	Cognitive knowledge (thinking)
Skilled craftsmen	Body (hands)	Physical skills (doing)
Manager "charioteers"	Emotion (heart)	Emotional attitude (feeling)

analysis, application, comprehension, evaluation, synthesis) and five attitudinal behaviors (characterization, organization, receiving, responding, valuing), he did not address the different types of psychomotor behavior (physical skills).

1962   Robert Mager: *Preparing Objectives for Programmed Instruction* (later became *Preparing Instructional Objectives*). Mager, with a wit and concision normally lacking in instructional circles, popularizes Bloom for the world of training and development by taking objectives out of the ivory tower and into the real world of the corporate practitioner. This is the text that sparked the modern boom in performance-improvement efforts focused on specific outcomes or objectives. Republished many times, this is still one of the standard texts.

1965   George Odiorne's *Management by Objectives* appears. Odiorne raises behavioral objectives to the organizational level and thereby helps launch a practice that will endure down to the present day. Building on Tyler's, Bloom's, and Mager's works on objectives, and aligning them with the concomitant rise of organizational development in the 1960s, Odiorne provided management with a reporting tool which, akin to accounting, permitted organizations to measure personal output and personal performance. MBOs are a forerunner and relative of modern competencies.

A Mager Sidebar

Mager is important enough to deserve a separate listing of his works. His books include (dates are of first edition):

Preparing Objectives for Programmed Instruction (1962) [later called *Preparing Instructional Objectives*]
Developing Vocational Instruction (1967)
Developing Attitude Toward Learning (1968)
Analyzing Performance Problems (1970)
Measuring Instructional Intent (1973)

His major works were collected and republished in a six-volume edition in 1984:

Analyzing Performance Problems
Goal Analysis
How to Turn Learners On Without Turning Them Off
Making Instruction Work
Measuring Instructional Results
Preparing Instructional Objectives

Core checklists and major points from his books are collected in *What Every Manager Should Know About Training* (1992).

1970   Robert Kibler et al: *Behavioral Objectives and Instruction.* A classic in the field.

1992   William Rothwell: *Mastering the Instructional Design Process: A Systematic Approach.* Part Three contains an excellent summary of research on learning objectives.

See also
Competencies

Content Design: Chunking and Sequencing

Content design is the art of outlining—of subdividing a course and then organizing it into proper pieces. It is system design, the art of grasping high level concepts, breaking up content into smaller units (chunking and decomposition of material into subclasses), and finally linking and relating these in a sequence and structure that makes sense to the end user. The process involves deconstructive as well as creative thinking.

I. DECOMPOSITION AND CHUNKING:
Differentiating Components

Decomposition: Separating into constituent parts.

—Webster's Dictionary

The Universe as Curriculum: Greek God as Instructional Designer

The Greek philosopher Anaxagoras believed that in the beginning a World Designer Mind ordered the universe by differentiating it into minute particles, then recombined these into a vast system. Anaxagoras's godlike World Mind was the first instructional designer, who differentiated, structured, and then sequenced the universe for humankind to wonder at and study as a "lifelong curriculum."

Chunk: A small but noteworthy piece of something, as in "a chunk of money."

—Webster's Dictionary

Aristotle, called by philosophers "the master of those who knew," best summed up the key steps in content design. The two steps in the process, he said, are:

1. Subdivide the material into the smallest intelligible chunks or units (today sometimes called "learning objects").

2. Link these units into a constituent logical structure (a hierarchical data structure, or tree diagram).

The subdividing process permits the logical *storage* of information, the linking process permits the ready *access* of that information.

Aristotle's first step is to spot subclasses in the material at hand. He cites as an example the subclasses of biology, where the genus (general *family*) of fish can be subdivided into specific subclasses, such as trout, bass, and salmon—and then further into *species* such as rainbow trout versus brook trout. The genus *animal* can similarly be subdivided into such subclasses as "human" versus chimpanzee, etc.

Aristotle goes on to describe how the entire domain of human knowledge, in fact, can be chunked into a hierarchy—a tree diagram upside down—with the most general family class at the top ("root"), reaching downwards through the branches and outwards through the subclasses and subsets (see Figure 2).

Aristotle's upside-down tree diagram may look simple, but it is a powerful tool. From Thomas Aquinas in the Middle Ages to Francis Bacon in the Renaissance, Denis Diderot in the Enlightenment, and John Dewey in modern times, systems thinkers and information architects have built upon it.

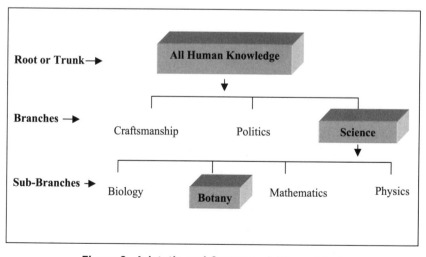

Figure 2. Aristotle and Systems: A Hierarchical Tree of Knowledge (Upside Down).

The real power behind the seemingly simple process of decomposition and hierarchical classification (top-down analysis followed by bottom-up synthesis) is that it provides a logical framework for a course. To illustrate how the concept of systems design lies at the heart of information design, let's look at the comparison of a corporate curriculum with the information structure of a typical book.

ROOT:	*Corporate Curriculum*	*Book*
BRANCHES:	Unit	Part
	Module	Chapter
	Lesson	Section
	Page (or Webscreen)	Page
	Line	Line

Information design for a course, as can be seen from this chart, is similar to the information design of a book or any other information vessel. Consider this brief story of the power of chunking in the evolution of information design throughout human history:

The Romans and the Sacrilegious Art of Chunking

Chunking is the key to powerful learning systems design, and yet has often been viewed as taboo.

■ *Moses and the Greeks: The Sacred Tablets and Scrolls Are Not to Be Chunked.* In the beginning was the Word and the Word was the sacred tablet and the scroll. As examples of the magical new medium and technology of writing, the tablet and the scroll were not to be chunked. Moses didn't chunk the stone tablets carrying the Ten Commandments nor did the Greeks chunk Plato's scrolls. For a thousand years the medium of writing remained sacred, magical, and off-limits to chunking.

■ *The Romans Invent the Heretical Art of Chunking.* Enter the Romans, who, being a generally uncultured, unruly, and unsuperstitious lot, held no beliefs about the sacredness of the medium of writing. They proceeded to chunk the scroll into "pages," which were then stitched together, thereby inventing the technology of the modern book. The book, they soon discovered, was fast, portable, and above all permitted random access to content. Chunking had finally begun its powerful march toward knowledge management. But one question remained: How was one to keep track of the content on all those pages?

■ *The Middle Ages: A Monk Invents the Search Engine.* Another thousand years would pass before an enterprising monk would invent the final piece in the chunking puzzle: the search engine. This was the "index" (literally "pointing finger") to the book. The index listed topics in a book alphabetically and, much like the modern database, created instant random access to any specific page or desired topic ("learning object"). A powerful new information system was born. Yet one element was still lacking: rapid dissemination of the book.

■ *The Renaissance: A Scientific Revolution from Chunking and Indexing.* Enter the invention of printing in 1450, which provided a high-volume global dissemination medium. At long last, small and timely pieces of scientific information could be stored (in an indexed book), retrieved, and disseminated. The scientific revolution of the Renaissance could now explode upon the modern world in full force, fueled largely by this new knowledge economy and its information machine—the chunked and indexed book flowing from printing presses all over Europe. The one-time stone tablet and the papyrus scroll, thanks to chunking, were now "pieces of information," forming a globally accessible database complete with search engine.

■ *Twenty-First Century: Chunking as Key to Learning Systems Design.* Our modern corporate learning systems are direct descendants of the Renaissance information system, with its powerful notion of chunking and indexing (meta-tagging) coupled with rapid dissemination. And all of this because an ancient Roman dared to chunk a scroll. The moral: Creative new information technology and information design always depends on "committing sacrilegious acts," going against established doctrines and traditions.

II. STRUCTURING AND SEQUENCING: Linking Components

Sequence: a connected series.

—Webster's Dictionary

All things were undiscriminated until
Intellect came and placed them in order.

              —Anaxagoras, teacher of Socrates, 450 B.C.

After content has been deconstructed into units, it needs to be structured and sequenced. This step is what Aristotle refers to as the linking or associating of components, and it can be of two types: simple linking (occurring within the same class, as in linking sales techniques with sales techniques) or composite linking (occurring between different classes, as in linking sales techniques with presentation techniques). In what follows we list seven types of sequencing.

Information Structures: Sequencing a Course

There are four basic structures of information: linear, branching, spiral, and scenario-based. Each of these structures comes into play where appropriate: linear for a course on a new product, branching for interactive simulations, spiral for a course on programming (circling upwards and building on what has already been learned), and scenario-based for a case study.

Built within these four structures are the varieties of actually sequencing material in a course. We list six basic ways of sequencing a course here.

Linear:

- Alphabetical
  Example: Online performance support systems. Typically alphabetical lists of topics or frequently asked questions.
- Chronological, Step-by-Step, or Procedural
  Example: Consultative selling skills (an overview, then stepwise instructions through the process).
- Known-to-Unknown
  Example: A suite of classes divided into "beginning, intermediate, and advanced" modules, each having as a prerequisite the previous class.

Branching:

- Core-and-Electives
  Example: Dividing a curriculum into required courses (core) and electives (branch-offs).

Spiral:

■ Easy-to-Difficult (Simple-to-Complex)
  Example: The typical way we learn a foreign language, beginning with easy words and progressing to more difficult ones. Sometimes called the cumulative approach or elaboration theory. (See Comenius.)

Scenario-based:

■ Solve-the-Problem
  Example: Simulations. A problem is presented to the student to capture attention and focus them on the steps necessary to solve it. This design structure supplies goal and motivation at the same time. It is sometimes referred to as problem-centered design or goal-driven scenarios and is a classic technique, one recommended by most major learning theorists. (See Comenius, Rousseau, and Dewey.)

None of these sequencing structures are absolutely distinct and separate from one another. Often more than one technique will be used in a course.

See also
Systems: An Architecture of Continuous Learning Systems

Evaluation: The Four Levels and ROI

Without measurement there is no performance improvement.
—W. Edwards Deming

Evaluation: the most powerful and underutilized tool in the entire arsenal of instructional systems design.
—Roger Chevalier

Kirkpatrick's Four Levels

Together with needs assessments, evaluations are among the most strategic tools available to the trainer or performance improvement practitioner. The evaluation of training programs involves four levels, which were originally suggested by Donald Kirkpatrick in the 1950s. In a series of four articles in *Training* magazine on "Techniques for Evaluating Training Programs," Kirkpatrick described how courses could be evaluated from four different perspectives (see Figure 3). The terms he used for these four levels were *reaction, learning, behavior*, and *results*. In what follows, these are referred to as *evaluation* (attitude), *knowledge* (cognitive), *application* (behavioral skills), and *impact* (financial results):

> *Level 1*: Evaluating the Course (How to Improve the Course)
> *Level 2*: Knowledge of What Was Taught (e.g., Certification of the Learner)
> *Level 3*: Applying It on the Job (Transfer to the Real World)
> *Level 4*: Impact on the Business (ROI and Bottom-line Profit)

LEVEL 1: Evaluating the Course (How to Improve the Course)

He made measurements everywhere, so that not one inch would be unaccounted for.
—Sherlock Holmes, *The Sign of the Four*, 1890

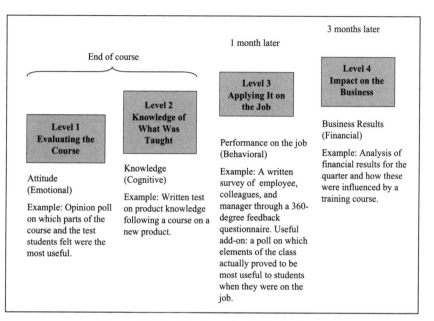

Figure 3. The Four Levels of Evaluation.

Level 1 evaluations survey student opinions on the course, including content, tests, and delivery.

Evaluation Source: Survey at the end of the course

Benefit: Gives directions on how course and delivery can be improved in the future.

Other Uses: Survey can be administered, not just at the end of the class, but each month, to determine what elements of the course are most useful on the job.

Challenge: Devising survey questions that are realistically helpful in evaluating how the course might be improved.

Teaching by lecture makes men mere scholars, but instructing by examination makes them learned: the student has the best chance of becoming actually great.

—Oliver Goldsmith, *An Enquiry into the*
Present State of Polite Learning in Europe, 1759

LEVEL 2: Knowledge of What Was Taught (Certification of the Learner)

Level 2 evaluations measure what the student has learned in the course.

Evaluation Source: Written exam at the end of the course.

Benefit: Allows for certifications or verifications of what was learned in the course. Benefits both learner and organization.

Other Uses: Evaluates indirectly the effectiveness of the organization's curriculum, tests, and delivery.

Challenge: Devising test questions that link the course to the real world of the job to be performed is sometimes difficult.

Test Scoring

Tests should not be graded "on a curve" (this is called "norm-referenced"), but rather on an objective scale, which is called "criterion-referenced." (A criterion is an objective standard.)

Evaluating is the most valuable treasure of all that we value: only through evaluation does value exist.

—Friedrich Nietzsche, *Thus Spoke Zarathustra*, 1883

LEVEL 3: Applying It on the Job (Transfer to the Real World)

Level 3 surveys participants one to three months after the course, to determine whether they are applying the new-found knowledge back on the job.

Evaluation Source: Several methods are used, including self-surveys as well as surveys of co-workers, managers, and direct reports. If all of these methods are utilized, Level 3 constitutes a 360-degree feedback survey.

Benefit: Level 3 feeds back valuable information on how effectively the learner is transferring what was learned to the job.

Other Uses: Level 3 evaluates not only the student's performance but also the effectiveness of the organization's courses, tests, and follow-on coaching and support programs.

Challenge: Designing the surveys so that they screen out factors other than training and measure only the impact of the course itself can be difficult.

Using Level 3 to Improve the Course

Level 3 surveys of learners, similar to Level 1 surveys, can be helpful in determining how courses, tests, and follow-on reinforcements can be improved. Simple Web surveys can be deployed, asking such direct questions as, "Of the 12 items you learned last month in class, which 3 do you find most useful on the job today?" Such surveys are not difficult to administer and can be of tremendous value to course developers. A side benefit of such surveys is that they also provide students with indirect reminders of what they were taught.

LEVEL 4: Impact on the Business (ROI and Bottom-Line Profit)

He whipped out a tape measure and hurried about the room—measuring, comparing, and evaluating.
                        —Sherlock Holmes, *The Sign of the Four*, 1890

Level 4 evaluation measures the cost savings and/or added revenue that can be attributed to a course. This level is the most difficult to establish, although there are several workarounds (see "Tips for Level 4" below).

Evaluation Source: There are numerous sources for Level 4, which is part of the problem in evaluating this level. Calculations should consider the cost of the training (easiest to compute), financial reports of the organization, and measures of on-the-job performance improvement of students following the course. Because on-the-job improvement is difficult to verify, this measure is often softened from a "proof" to a "correlation"—see "Tips for Level 4" below.

Benefit: Measures bottom-line results (company profits or return on investment) resulting from the training. If these can't be confirmed, there are other measures possible: cost reductions, reductions in cycle time, time-to-market, or time-to-competency.

Other Uses: Level 4 indicates not only the training department's contribution to the company's bottom line, but also the organization's overall effectiveness—which can be motivational feedback for employers and employees alike. Results should be celebrated and rewarded.

Challenge: This level of evaluation is time-consuming and costly to perform. ROI due to training is difficult to substantiate for there are many factors at work. As we've stated, it may be more realistic to demonstrate plausible cases or correlations in data trends (see Tips below).

TIP   **Tips for Level 4**

■ *Cluster soft skills into a group.* It is particularly difficult to evaluate the financial impact of soft skills courses. *Tip*: Instead of trying to measure the impact of, say, listening skills on your company's bottom line, group this class with other classes, such as selling techniques, and proposal writing. Then measure their *combined* impact on the bottom line by clustering them as a mini-curriculum called, for instance, "Effective Selling." The skill cluster functions more like a competency, and therefore can be more readily correlated to the bottom line.

■ *Speak of retention and satisfaction levels.* If hard data is unavailable for determining the financial impact of training, reach for softer data. Look instead, for instance, at "employee retention levels" as measured by turnover, or at "employee satisfaction levels." Ask questions such as "Do you feel prepared to return and apply these skills on the job?" or "Was the course worthwhile?" These factors can be viewed as "key differentiators," and therefore as a competitive advantage for the firm.

■ *Use opinion surveys to project correlated approximations of financial impact.* If no Level 4 financial data is available, John Noonan has proposed an inventive solution. This is not as strange as it sounds at first. He suggests projecting Level 4 financial impact from Level 1 attitude surveys containing such questions as "Rate your productivity, following the training, on the tasks that utilize what was presented in the course." Although the method is too detailed to reproduce in its entirety here, it basically approximates financial payback by extrapolating from field surveys filled out by learners. Not billed as ROI, but rather as plausible cases and ranges of magnitude, and with the appropriate disclaimers ("we're building a business case, not trying to publish in an academic journal"), Noonan's "directional indicators" can still be useful to managers in terms of deciding whether the training was effective or not. If the only alternative is to produce no Level 4 results at all, Noonan's suggestion is an interesting and creative one.

■ *Tackle the easiest first.* ROI is gathered from four sources; arrange these from easy to most difficult and tackle the easiest first:

　　Cost Savings: This is the simplest ROI factor to link to training because it involves fewer variables than do revenue or earnings estimates. This factor is most often cited when making the case for Web courses, which will presumably eliminate the cost of trainers, classrooms, travel, and hotels.

Time Savings: Reduction in time-to-competency, time-to-market, cycle time, etc.

Increase in Revenue (Sales): More difficult ROI factor to link to training because there are more variables.

Increase in Earnings (Profit): The most complex ROI factor to link to training, for it involves the most variables.

Is There a Level 5?

Sometimes a Level 5 is suggested, which generally involves ROI, but this is essentially a component of Level 4. Whether it constitutes Level 4 or 5 is purely academic. The chief point is getting there, not whether you call it 4 or 5.

Before You Evaluate, Preevaluate (Don't Forget Level 0)

Level 0 is what I call evaluation *before* any training has been done. It is a snapshot of current-state performance. You may already have done this in your front-end needs assessment, but if you didn't, and you plan on evaluating after the new initiative, then it is imperative that you establish current-state benchmarks before deploying the new solution. This may sound obvious, but astonishingly few corporations do this. In the rush to deploy new and better solutions based on technology, people overlook this first crucial step. Establish current-state baselines before you proceed. You will be richly rewarded.

The Four Levels Are Four Phases

Traditionally the first two evaluation levels are taken at the end of the class in the form of a survey of student attitudes (plus an exam). The third level is gathered on the job a month or two later, and the fourth level is generally calculated at the end of the following financial quarter. Thus the levels are actually spread out over time, and they should perhaps better be referred to as the "four phases" of evaluation.

The Origin of the Four Levels: The Domains of Learning

Although Kirkpatrick makes no reference to Benjamin Bloom's earlier work on learning objectives (see Fastpaths 1956, Bloom), Kirkpatrick essentially translates Bloom's three kinds of learning (knowledge, skills, and attitudes) into three levels of evaluation. "Attitudes" become Level 1 evaluation (opinion); "knowledge" becomes Level 2 evaluation (cognitive tests); and "skills" on-the-job become Level 3 evaluation. Kirkpatrick then adds a fourth level, namely financial impact of the training. The following chart summarizes the comparison:

Bloom's Three Learning Domains

1. Emotional (Attitude)
2. Mental (Knowledge)
3. Physical (Skills)

Kirkpatrick's Four Evaluation Levels

1. Emotional (Attitude toward the course)
2. Mental (Tests in class)
3. Physical (Transfer to on-the-job skills)
4. Financial (Additional)

FASTPATHS

1956   Benjamin Bloom: *Taxonomy of Educational Objectives.* Bloom's three domains of learning objectives are precursors of Kirkpatrick's four levels of evaluation.

1959   Donald Kirkpatrick's series of four articles in *Training* magazine on "Techniques for Evaluating Training Programs," in which he formulates the four levels of evaluation.

1971   James Block: *Mastery Learning: Theory and Practice.*

1973   Robert Mager: *Measuring Instructional Intent.* A classic text on testing and measurement. Republished numerous times.

1989   Dana and James Robinson: *Training for Impact: How to Link Training to Business Needs and Measure the Results.*

1994   Donald Kirkpatrick: *Evaluating Training Programs: The Four Levels.*

1995   John Noonan: *Elevators: How to Move Training Up from the Basement.* See his chapter on "Evaluation," with its creative suggestions for Level 1 surveys to produce Level 4 approximations in an organization.

1997   Jack Phillips: *Handbook of Training Evaluation and Measurement Methods.* One of several titles by Phillips, who specializes in evaluation.

1999   Odin Westgaard: *Tests That Work.*

1999   Richard Swanson and E. Holton: *Results: How to Assess Performance, Learning, and Perceptions in Organizations.*

2000   Jac Fitz-enz: *The ROI of Human Capital.*

2002   Judith Hale: *Performance-Based Evaluation: Tools and Techniques to Measure the Impact of Training.* Hale, an expert on evaluation, re-emphasizes the crucial distinction between academic knowledge-based tests (Level 2) and actual on-the-job performance-based evaluations (Level 3).

> ***See also***
> Return on Investment and Cost-Benefit Analysis

What gets measured, gets done.

—Roger Chevalier, 2002

Twenty Seconds into the Future

The Architecture of Continuous Learning Systems

As a system I am not totally perfect, but parts of me are excellent.
—Ashleigh Brilliant, 1979

All right, everybody line up alphabetically—according to height.
—Casey Stengel, Manager, New York Yankees, 1950

Definition of Systems

A system, according to *Webster's*, is an assemblage of objects united by a regular interdependence or interaction of the parts. Deriving from the Greek and meaning "to place together," a system constitutes an organic or organized whole comprised of multiple sections. Examples of systems would be the solar system, the human nervous system, a curriculum system, an organizational system, or simply the Rolodex on your desk. Systems are built from interlocking parts, which are often in motion. Thus planets in star systems link with one another through moving gravity fields, organs in your body connect with one another through organic tissue and nerve impulses, and courses in a curriculum system connect with one another through cross-referencing and hyperlinks.

Systems thinking isn't new. Long before systems thinking came about in technology and organizations, there was systems thinking in theology, philosophy, medicine, and astronomy. In 400 B.C., the Greek physician Hippocrates described the human body as a system and in 350 B.C. Aristotle viewed all human knowledge as one vast hierarchical system. In A.D. 1200, the theologian Thomas Aquinas, building directly on Aristotle, turned systems thinking into a fine art with a vast system of scholastic philosophy mirroring the towering Gothic cathedrals of his time. And the Renaissance of the sixteenth and seventeenth centuries produced the astronomical systems of Copernicus and Galileo. By the time of World War II, systems thinking had entered the realm of technology in the form of computerized anti-aircraft guns, and about the same time, had also started to define our thinking about organizations, with the sociotechnical movement in England. In each and every case, the system was driven by the core vision of *an assemblage of complex interlocking parts in motion.*

The Organization as System: Closed Machine Systems vs. Open Living Systems

The secret of any method is to arrange all facts into a system.
—Descartes, *Rules for Direction of Mind,* 1630

There are two types of organizational systems, namely machine systems and living system. One way of expressing the difference is through the metaphors of the machine and the garden—the one mechanical, the other organic. Machine systems are closed, and are based on cybernetics theory (small machines steering large machines). Living systems, on the other hand, are open and based on organic theories of self-organization. Modern systems thinking tends to embrace both of these theories.

Machine Systems Theory

Originating in the seventeenth century celestial mechanics of Newton's astronomical system, machine systems were brought down to earth in the twentieth century by the cybernetic thinkers Norbert Wiener and William Ashby. During the 1940s, both these men explored the crucial role of *feedback* and of *servo-mechanisms* in machine systems. Servo-mechanisms are the small servant machines that play steersman to the main system, course-correcting the system so that it performs optimally (see Figure 4). For example, governors controlled early steam engines, thermostats controlled furnaces, and, in a similar manner, today's cruise controls control cars, automatic pilots steer aircraft, and automatic focus devices focus digital camcorders. In organizations, the governors correspond to the managers—steering and course-correcting the entire organization.

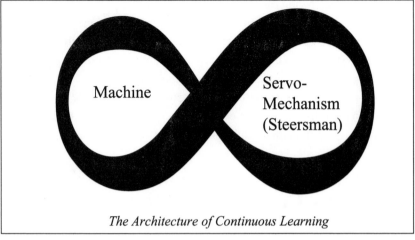

The Architecture of Continuous Learning

Figure 4. Machine Systems Design.

Living Systems Theory

Where machine systems are "planned" systems, living systems are "self-organized," developing organically over time. Open systems theory implies all things link up and influence one another, in all directions (easy to say, but challenging to work with). Drawing heavily on Aristotle, Goethe, Herder, and Hegel, the biologist Ludwig Bertalanffy developed living systems theory in Austria in the 1920s (see Figure 5). The theory later became known as "open" systems and also "general" systems theory. His research, focusing on self-evolving systems from single-cell organisms to entire organizations, studied how higher, second-order living systems (managers in an organization) controlled lower, primary-order systems (employees). Social psychologists Kurt Lewin and Gregory Bateson followed Bertalanffy and extended the metaphor to learning, studying the interaction between the small-group learning by employees and higher level learning by managers (and trainers). Not only did each group have to learn from each other, but the trainers in particular had to "learn how to learn" (i.e., learn how to teach), which Bateson called *deutero-learning*, and what we today call meta-learning (the organization "learning how to teach"). The theory has continued to evolve, particularly in the organizational systems thinking of Wheatley and Capra (see Fastpaths 1992 and 1996).

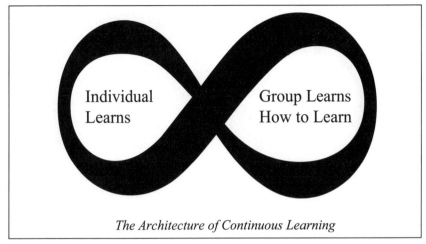

The Architecture of Continuous Learning

Figure 5. Living Systems Design.

Double Loop Learning: The Organization Starts to Learn

"Learning how to learn" will be the first order of business.
—Don Marchand and F. Horton: *Infotrends*, 1986

At the heart of and connecting both machine systems and living systems is the process of double-loop learning. The concept derives originally from Bateson and Ashby, and was further amplified as a metaphor for organizational models by Schon and Argyris (see 1974 in Fastpaths below). Double-loop learning is the theory of how and where *individual learning meets organizational learning.* The term itself derives from the "feedback loops" drawn on engineering drawings and circuit designs. Translated into the training realm, the first feedback loop refers to the learning done by a student (from feedback provided on tests), whereas the second loop refers to the learning done by the trainer (from course evaluations). Thus, as the student learns how to perform better, the trainer learns how to train better (as both a designer and deliverer of training). In fact, the trainer is practicing what might be called meta-training, learning how to learn AND train better. Learner and trainer are intertwined in an ongoing *system that is continuously improving itself.* The two feedback loops joining the two participants in the system are what

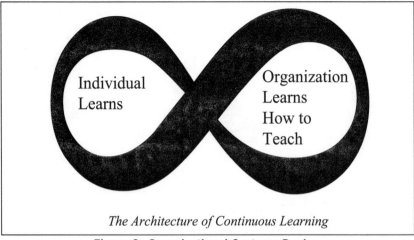

The Architecture of Continuous Learning

Figure 6. Organizational Systems Design.

we call double-loop learning (see Figure 6). This lies at the heart of organizational systems design.

Knowledge Orbits: Twin Feedback Loops

The twin feedback loops in a continuous learning organization could be diagrammed by highlighting the distinctions in the two force fields of performance, as follows:

First Loop Learning	*Second Loop Learning*
Student learns	Teacher learns
Feedback loop to individual	Feedback loop to organization
Tactical	Strategic
Course-based	Curriculum-based

The twin loops include the following further distinctions:

First Loop Learning	*Second Loop Learning*
Feedback: Test scores	Feedback: Curriculum evaluations
Individual context	Group context
Result: Learning	Result: Learning about learning
Impact: Individual performance	Impact: Organizational performance

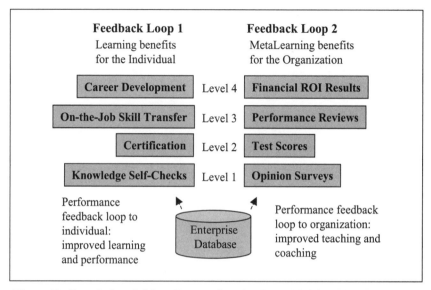

Figure 7. Knowledge Orbits: Connecting the Force Fields of Performance.

Whether viewed within the context of machine systems or living systems (for it exists in both), the double-loop learning process connects Loop 1 student learning with Loop 2 teacher learning—through *knowledge orbits*, information circulating in a performance force field. Figure 7 diagrams this process and highlights the benefits for each side within the continuous learning system.

Extreme Learning Systems: Enabling the Vision

There's magic in the Web.

—Shakespeare, *Othello*, 1604

Learning *ex Machina:* The Web

With the advent of the Web, and what are currently called learning management systems, the architecture of continuous learning systems is slowly being put into place. For the first time in history, the vision of double loop learning—with its continually spinning feedback loops to both individual and organization—can become a reality. Such systems provide trainers with reporting tools, which can give a history and instant snapshot of the effectiveness of training initiatives. Learning management systems are to performance what the instant replay is to professional sports—providing instant feedback to support both accountability and accuracy in the training profession. This, coupled with high speed, globally accessible knowledge bases, and delivery networks, means we are entering an era of "extreme learning." But infrastructure, we must always remind ourselves, is not enough. If organizations are going to put the vision into practice, they will have to master content management, learning strategy, and strategic implementation as well—all within a systems context.

When we try to pick out anything by itself, we find it hitched to everything else in the universe.

—John Muir, 1869

FASTPATHS

1903 Frederick Taylor: *Shop Management.* Speaks to the systems side of manufacturing, and prescribes the chunking of system operations into component sub-processes for task analysis and performance improvement efforts. Taylor anticipates Deming's TQM in the 1980s as well as Michael Hammer's process reengineering in the 1990s.

1912 Alexander Bogdanov's pioneering *Tektology* ("the structure of systems") appears in Russia, defining organizational form as "the totality of connections among systemic elements." Initiates the field of living or open systems design (how living organisms learn), which Bertalanffy (1950) will pursue.

1933 George Humphrey: *The Nature of Learning in its Relation to the Living System.* Humphrey applied early systems theory to psychology. Influenced by Einstein's relativity theory and the search for a unified field theory, Humphrey suggests that psychological experience equates to a four-dimensional space-time continuum in which learning depends more on the time dimension, while perception rests on the spatial dimension.

1936 Arthur Lovejoy: *The Great Chain of Being,* the classic study of systems thinking from Plato through Aquinas to the Romantics.

1947 W. Ross Ashby: "Principles of the Self-Organizing Dynamic System" appears in the *Journal of General Psychology.* Anticipates his book (see 1952).

1948 Norbert Wiener: *Cybernetics: Or the Control and Communication in the Animal and the Machine.* Along with Ashby's book (1952), one of the two founding texts of modern systems thinking.

1950   Ludwig von Bertalanffy (1901–1972): "Theory of Open Systems in Physics and Biology" in *Science* magazine. Bertalanffy, a transplanted Austrian biologist who had been influenced by the Viennese Gestalt school of psychology (a "systems" view of psychology) and had already published in German in the 1920s, becomes a leader in the field of "open" living systems. Such "living" or "organic" systems (stemming from the thought of Aristotle and Goethe) were opposed to the architectural "machine" systems of Wiener (1948) and

> "Living systems" and "machine systems" are two major models of systems thinking.

Ashby (1952), which were "closed" systems. These two opposing types of systems thinking would continue at odds down through the latter half of the twentieth century, as witnessed by MIT's Senge (captive to the machines systems vision of Forrester) versus Capra and Wheatley (promoting the organic view of organizations). In the twenty-first century, the two theories are now coalescing.

1952   W. Ross Ashby: *Design for a Brain*. British theorist, initiates "machine" view of systems, which will culminate in Forrester's and MIT's view of systems. Ashby, along with Wiener, develops the notion of feedback and of single- and double-loop learning (the latter including learning about learning). Together with Wiener (1948) Ashby is one of the two founders of modern systems thinking. In 1956 he publishes *An Introduction to Cybernetics.*

1954   International Society for the System Sciences is founded (ISSS). Its motto is a definition of system: "Elements working together as a whole." See www.ISSS.org

1961   Jay Forrester, MIT professor of machine systems theory, publishes *Industrial Dynamics.*

1962   Robert Gagne edits anthology *Psychological Principles in System Development*, which includes key chapter by Meredith Crawford on systems thinking in instructional design— including her proto-outline of an ADDIE model for instructional design (developed during the 1950s by the U.S. military). The method would be popularized in 1975 in a series of white papers.

> My mother, whose views on education were remarkably strict, brought me up to be extremely short-sighted; it is part of her system.
>
> —Heroine in Oscar Wilde's
> *The Importance of Being Earnest*, 1895

1962   Thomas Kuhn: *Structure of Scientific Revolutions*. Its key concept of paradigm (mental model), with its example of the revolutionary shift in thinking from Aristotle to Newton, is directly related to systems thinking. (See Paradigm)

1965   Charles Kepner and Benjamin Tregoe: *The Rational Manager: A Systematic Approach to Problem Solving and Decision Making*. Classic performance improvement model built on problem solving.

1968   Ludwig von Bertalanffy: *General Systems Theory* (a collection of essays from the 1930s onwards). Bertalanffy's "general" systems theory equates to "open" or "living" systems theory.

1972   George Klir (ed.): *Trends in General Systems Theory*. Papers on the development of systems thinking across several disciplines.

1972   Paul Friesen: *Designing Instruction: A Systems Approach Using Programmed Instruction*. Well-written summary of PI system.

1972   Gregory Bateson: *Steps to an Ecology of Mind*, early precursor to learning systems theory. Formulates a theory of deutero-learning or "learning how to learn," which is very close to Ashby's earlier double-loop learning theory (1952): While the individual learns, the organization learns HOW to learn.

1973   William Gray and Nicholas Rizzo (eds.): *Unity Through Diversity: A Festschrift for Ludwig von Bertalanffy*.

1973   Fred Emery and Eric Trist: *Toward a Social Ecology*. Since the 1950s these two British experts, building on Bertalanffy's work on open systems, had been propounding a practical dynamic systems view of organizational development. Stressed the socio-technical side of organizational design as opposed to scientific Taylorism (see Fastpaths 1987, Weisbord).

1974   Donald Schon and Chris Argyris: *Theory in Practice*. Formulate theory of double loop learning with application to organizations, based on the theories of Wiener and Ashby.

1975   ADDIE is born, the system employed by instructional designers. Instructional Systems Design (ISD) is officially launched as a model by Florida State University (and simultaneously by the U.S. military)

1978   Robert Lilienfeld: *The Rise of Systems Theory*. Good summary of movement.

1978   James Miller: *Living Systems*. Exhaustive study of the topic (of organic, open systems).

1978   Walter Dick and Lou Carey: *The Systematic Design of Instruction*. Still an important textbook in the field.

1979   Douglas Hofstadter: *Goedel, Escher, Bach*. Focuses on the feedback loops in systems.

1985   Robert Tannenbaum et al.: *Human Systems Development: New Perspectives on People and Organizations.*

1987   Marvin Weisbord: *Productive Workplaces.*

1988   Robert Wright: *Three Scientists and their Gods: Looking for Meaning in an Age of Information.* (See Knowledge Management.)

1990   Charles Handy: *The Age of Unreason* (on the learning organization).

1990   Peter Senge: *The Fifth Discipline: The Art and Practice of the Learning Organization.*

1990   Richard Pascale: *Managing on the Edge: How the Smartest Companies Use Conflict to Stay Ahead.* Chapter on "the two faces of learning" distinguishes little "l" learning (maximization) from Big "L" Learning (metamization).

1991   George Richardson: *Feedback Thought in Social Science and Systems Theory.* A superb study of systems thinking across multiple disciplines.

1992   William Rothwell and H. Kazanas: *Mastering the Instructional Design Process: A Systematic Approach.* Excellent summary of instructional design processes and theories. One of the best.

1992   Margaret Wheatley: *Leadership and the New Science: Discovering Order in a Chaotic World.* An "organic" systems view of organizations.

1996   Chris Argyris and Donald Schon. *Organizational Learning II.*

1996   Fritjof Capra: *The Web of Life: A New Scientific Understanding of Living Systems.* Good summary of the history of organic systems thinking (as well as of Ashby and Wiener's machine systems models).

1998   Stephen Haines: *Systems Thinking and Learning.* A good summary of living systems theory as applied to organizations.

Systems: The Experts Speak Out

Knowledge of the human body depends upon knowledge of the whole man.

—Hippocrates on Medicine, 400 B.C.

The first question is whether there is a system.

—Francis Bacon, 1620

Without a system, it would be easy for elements to be omitted and for failure to step in.

—Johann Comenius, 1650

I speak of a system of government.
—Spinoza, *Political Treatise*, 1677

The center of the world system is unmovable.
—Newton, *The System of the World*, 1687

Observe how system into system runs . . .
—Alexander Pope, 1734

In nature everything depends on everything else.
—Diderot, 1750

The principles of a system, which I shall explain and examine.
—Adam Smith, *Wealth of Nations*, 1776

Star systems, part of still vaster systems.
—Kant, 1790

To catch a system by the tail is like catching a lizard—the whole truth escapes and leaves the tail in your hand.
—Turgenev, 1850

Naturalists arrange species, genera, and families into what is called a Natural System.
—Charles Darwin, *The Origin of Species*, 1859

Problems that are created by our current level of thinking can't be solved on that same level of thinking.
—Albert Einstein, 1910

In the past, man was first; in the future, the system will be first.
—Frederick Taylor, *The Principles of Scientific Management*, 1911

Every system is inevitably incomplete: it will contain certain statements that cannot be proved within that system.
—Kurt Goedel, *The Incompleteness Theorem*, 1930

Systems are man-made organisms.
—Robert Gagne, 1962

Systematic: carrying out a design with thoroughness and regularity.
—Webster's Dictionary, 1982

A snowflake is itself a particular system.
—Paul Davies, *The Edge of Infinity,* 1990

Questioner: "I'm worried about the tail wagging the dog."
Systems Expert: "The tail is the dog."

—Anonymous

II. GENERAL CONCEPTS
A to Z

This learning, what a thing it is!
—Shakespeare, *The Taming of the Shrew*, 1594

Action Learning

Action learning, originally called "action research," is a tool of organizational development created in the 1940s by Kurt Lewin in the United States and Reginald Revans in England. In many ways a precursor of Japanese quality circles in the 1980s, action learning consists of small-group efforts in an organization to solve problems at a grass roots level. Designated teams work together to set tasks, come up with solutions, and effect change from below. The term sometimes is used in a much broader sense to simply mean "learning on the job."

FASTPATHS

1948   Kurt Lewin: *Resolving Social Conflicts: Selected Papers on Group Dynamics.*

1951   Kurt Lewin: *Field Theory in Social Science: Selected Theoretical Papers.*

1969   Alfred Marrow: *The Practical Theorist: The Life and Work of Kurt Lewin.*

1980   Reginald Revans: *Action Learning: New Techniques for Management.*

1982   Reginald Revans: *The Origins and Growth of Action Learning.*

1983   Mike Pedler (ed.): *Action Learning in Practice.* Anthology of articles on the British action learning movement started by Revans.

1987   Marvin Weisbord: *Productive Workplaces.* A readable history of organizational development, including action learning.

2000   David Garvin: *Learning in Action: A Guide to Putting the Learning Organization to Work.*

> **See also**
> Learning Organization
> Lessons Learned
> Organizational Development (OD)

Adult Learning

A wise man increaseth in learning.
> —Bible, *Proverbs* 1:5

Education never ends, Watson.
> —Sherlock Holmes, *The Adventure of the Red Circle,* 1911

Definition and Background

Adult learning, or andragogy (from Greek, meaning "adult learning"), refers to the principles and practices involved in how adults acquire and use knowledge, skills, and attitudes. In the United States, andragogy's roots reach back to the mid-1800s, when it was called vocational education and the new industrialism first brought in night schools, continuing education programs, and correspondence courses. The academic theory and discipline of adult learning began in the United States in the 1920s with the works of Eduard Lindeman, and continued in the second half of the century with the works of Malcolm Knowles.

Principles

The two chief principles of adult learning are self-direction and relevancy.

■ *Self-Direction.* Adult instruction should be customized as much as possible to the individual learner, with the trainer acting more as facilitator than teacher. Courses should be self-paced, and the learner's experience should be utilized wherever possible as a resource in the learning.

■ *Relevancy.* Adult learning should have a real-world focus and be rooted in what educators call "authentic" tasks. Because adults have more life and work experience than youth, they are less inclined to take the teacher's word at face value. Courses need to relate directly to the adult's life situation or to their work. Adults also respond better to problem-based courses than to lectures. Whenever possible, courses should utilize real-life scenarios and students should work on their own projects—geared to their own interests and personal goals. Standardized tests should be supplemented by self-tests (pre- as well as post-), which are more motivating.

Course Design

In sum, adult learning theory stresses the importance of *learner-relevance* at every point in the learning process. Self-planning beforehand, self-assessment afterwards, and authentic, action-based tasks in between constitute the most powerful learning pathway. In addition to self-directed learning, adult learning stresses the importance, where appropriate, of collaborative learning as well.

Lifelong Learning and the Spectrum of Learning

The aim of life is self-development. Most people forget this.
—Oscar Wilde, 1890

In the twenty-first century adult learning has been extended to yet a third learning phase—what the Germans call "gerontagogy," what the French call "the third age," and what Americans call "learning for seniors."

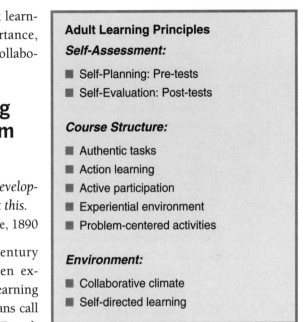

Adult Learning Principles

Self-Assessment:

- Self-Planning: Pre-tests
- Self-Evaluation: Post-tests

Course Structure:

- Authentic tasks
- Action learning
- Active participation
- Experiential environment
- Problem-centered activities

Environment:

- Collaborative climate
- Self-directed learning

The Spectrum of Learning

Pedagogy	*Andragogy*	*Gerontagogy*
Child learning	Adult learning	Senior learning

The concept of the learning spectrum raises the concept of adult learning to part of a larger whole—namely the concept of lifelong learning. Reaching back 2,400 years to ancient Greece, when Socrates taught Plato on the stone steps of the marketplace, lifelong learning is also very much the future of the twenty-first century. And within this spectrum adult learning, which is destined to play a major role, is only just beginning to take advantage of modern learning and performance principles.

FASTPATHS

Seek knowledge throughout your life, from cradle to grave.
—Mohammed, A.D. 600

1607   Apprenticeship programs in Jamestown Colony, Virginia (ancestor of vocational-technical schools).

1800s   The growth of home correspondence schools for adults, the beginnings of adult "distance learning."

1831   First tax-supported public library established, in New Hampshire.

1833   The German Alexander Kapp, in a commentary on Plato's theory of education in *The Republic,* coins the term *Andragogik* (adult education).

1851   James Hudson: *The History of Adult Education.* Republished several times since.

1860   Samuel Smiles: *Self-Help.* Founds the self-help (self-directed learning) movement for adults, in England. (See Carnegie, 1936.)

1873   First university extension classes taught at Oxford and Cambridge.

1924   Eugen Rosenstock's *Andragogik* appears in Germany. Although the term had been coined a century earlier, andragogy's main impact wasn't felt in Germany until the need to rebuild its adult workforce following the devastations of World War I.

1926   In the United States, Eduard Lindeman publishes *The Meaning of Adult Education.*

1926   American Association for Adult Education is organized, dedicated to enhancing the field of adult learning. See Web site www.aace.org. Still publishes *Adult Learning* journal.

1927   Eduard Lindeman and Martha Anderson publish *Education Through Experience*, a summary of the adult education movement going on in Germany under the Labor Academy throughout the early 1920s.

1928   Edward Thorndike: *Adult Learning.* The views of a founding behaviorist.

1936   Dale Carnegie publishes *How to Win Friends and Influence People*. This Depression-era best-seller single-handedly founded the self-directed adult learning movement in the United States. Carnegie's discovery of the power of directed praise, for instance, anticipates not only *The One Minute Manager's* "one-minute praisings" of the 1980s but also other major motivation theories. His belief in the importance of emotional attitude (the need to "nourish self-esteem") directly anticipates Maslow's category of self-esteem in his hierarchy of needs of the 1950s.

1950   Malcolm Knowles (1913–1997), so-called father of adult education in the United States, publishes his book *Informal Adult Education*. Building on the work of Lindeman before him, Knowles lays out adult learning principles in a series of books:

1954   *Teaching Adults in Informal Courses*
1960   *Handbook of Adult Education*
1962   *The Adult Education Movement in the United States*
1969   *Higher Adult Education*
1970   *The Modern Practice of Adult Education: From Pedagogy to Andragogy*
1973   *The Adult Learner: A Neglected Species*
1975   *Self-Directed Learning: A Guide for Learners and Teachers*
1977   *Adult Development and Learning: A Handbook*
1984   *Andragogy in Action*

1961   Britain's Open University (university without walls) begins operation.
1961   Cyril Houle: *The Inquiring Mind.* A study of the adult learner.
1983   David Kolb: *Experiential Learning.*
1988   Ron Zemke: "30 Things We Know for Sure About Adult Learning," *Training,* July 1988.
1995   Ron Zemke: "Adult Learning: What Do We Know for Sure?" *Training,* June 1995.

See also
Distance Learning
Learning Style

Advance Organizer

An advance organizer is an introduction or table of contents to a course. It can also refer to an abstract, a general overview, preliminary instructions, topics to be covered, course outline, or a study plan. Philosophers have long used the Greek term *propaedeutic* (pre-pedagogical or pre-teaching comments) for this concept, but educator David Ausubel came up with "advance organizer" in 1963, and it has remained a stock term in certain instructional design circles ever since. Note that the concept of an introductory overview represents the first of Herbart's standard four-step process for building any course.

FASTPATHS

1963   David Ausubel: *Psychology of Meaningful Verbal Learning*

See also
Herbart

Behaviorism

A man of fact and calculations, ready to weigh and measure any parcel of human nature!
—Description of Mr. Gradgrind in Charles Dickens's *Hard Times*, 1854

All human performance, when objectified in units of space and time, follows certain laws.
—E. L. Thorndike, Behaviorist, 1901

Behaviorism is a twentieth-century movement in psychology away from the nineteenth century's descriptive studies of inner states of consciousness toward a scientific study of outward behavior and physical actions. Strongly influenced by nineteenth century laboratory science, behaviorism prides itself on being logical and precise, studying behavior in terms of absolutely observable and measurable acts. Only what people are observed to be doing counts; it is off-limits for behaviorists to talk about "thinking" or about the head. Instead of stating quite simply that they are "training an employee in a new habit," for instance, behaviorists state that they are "conditioning a reflex response associated with a specific environmental stimulus." Behaviorism prides itself in being the "pure science" of habit formation.

How does behaviorism inculcate new habits (or help us unlearn bad ones)? The answer is that it conditions, modifies, and shapes new behavior patterns through reinforcement, meaning through either reward or punishment. Early behaviorism claimed, in fact, that all emotions (except fear, love, and anger) could be conditioned or habitualized by simply reinforcing the desired emotion.

Influenced by Pavlov's "classical conditioning" of dogs in Russia around 1900 (see Fastpaths 1900, Pavlov), behaviorism was introduced into the United States in the early 1900s by John B. Watson. By the 1940s it was the only learning theory around, being the major force behind all skills training during World War II. During the 1950s it was promoted heavily by B. F. Skinner, who came up with the variant of behaviorism called process-oriented or "operant" conditioning (see Fastpaths 1938, Skinner), which was a refinement on Pavlov's classical conditioning methods. Using the newly developed teaching machine with its "programmed instruction," Skinner stated that skills should be taught in small steps. In this version, even very complex behaviors were viewed as simply a series of observable, mechanically linked (or "chained") events, each subevent being appropri-

> Ninety percent of hitting is mental, the other half is physical.
>
> —Yogi Berra, 1958

ately "associated" with the next. The only task was to "condition" (habitualize) the employee to the desired sequence of these steps. In this fashion, behaviorism held sway virtually unchallenged in corporate training departments until the 1990s (when cognitivism started to make its first inroads).

Behaviorism has been an enormous force in the training, learning, and performance world over the past century, and in spite of often overstating its case, it has provided a constantly healthy corrective to more abstract theories of learning. In fact, many of its learning principles, including those of "programmed instruction," still hold true for today's Web-based courses (small steps for small screens). Today, however, most trainers and performance consultants embrace what could be called a blended form of learning, or "cognitive behaviorism," rather than either behaviorism or cognitivism. (See Cognitivism section for a chart contrasting behaviorism with cognitivism.)

"Behaviorism" Is Often a Blanket Term for "Effective Training"

In the real world "behaviorism," because it has reigned unchallenged in departments of training for fifty years, is often used as a blanket term to mean simply "training with impact" (as in "our course results in real behavior change."). It does not always convey the precise meaning and the academic differentiation from cognitivism that we are making here. Often, in fact, it is referring to what is actually "cognitive behaviorism."

FASTPATHS

1690 The modern discipline of psychology is born when the English philosopher John Locke comes up with the theory of association, which will dominate the beginnings of psychology in the 1700s and 1800s and be revived yet again in the twentieth century by the behaviorists. The psychologist's task, according to Locke, is to discover how the units of experience (perceptions, memories, impressions, reflexes, and habits) are connected with one another, and how these in turn become combined into complex chains of ideas and actions.

1870   Wilhelm Wundt's *Physiological Psychology* appears in Germany, announcing the arrival of experimental psychology—as a scientific discipline separate from philosophy. Much like the modern behavioral-cognitive psychology, which was to come 100 years later, Wundt stakes out a claim to a scientific field that will "examine the points of contact between external AND internal life."

1875   William James establishes an experimental psychology laboratory at Harvard. Formal birthdate of modern psychology in the United States. James had studied with Wundt.

1880   Wilhelm Wundt establishes a psychology lab in Leipzig, Germany.

1890   William James's *Principles of Psychology* appears. A groundbreaking textbook in the new field of psychology by one of the founders of modern psychology.

1892   The American Psychological Association (APA) is founded, with an initial membership of thirty, including William James.

1898   Edward Thorndike (1874–1949) publishes *Animal Intelligence,* which helps found Behaviorism in the United States. Thorndike, a student of the pragmatism of William James as well as of the empirical psychology of the German Wundt, postulates a theory of learning that will dominate all others for almost a century, namely the notion that actions (responses) can be associated or causally "connected" with sense impressions (stimuli). *Example:* a bell rings and you do nothing; second step: a bell rings and your favorite dessert is brought in; the third time,

> The birth of psychology lays the foundation for organizational development and instructional design.

when the bell rings, you salivate (even though the dessert has been withheld). You have "learned" something (how to salivate at the sound of a bell) through a "stimulus response" process. The behaviorists were off and running to their labs and their largely "transhuman subjects" of white mice, city pigeons, and rats, and a movement was born: Behaviorist Psychology.

Thorndike also postulated what he called the *law of readiness,* namely the notion that the learner must be motivated if he is to learn (an insight as old as Plato, and still valid). This will lead directly to all current problem-centered and goal-centered design

> No learning can take place without motivation.

in adult learning. Thorndike also postulated the *law of exercise*: practicing a response, with reinforcement, is essential if we are to acquire a new skill.

1900   Pavlov's revolutionary experiments in Russia prove Thorndike's theories. The process went as follows: Meat was placed in a dog's mouth and caused the dog to salivate, exhibiting an instinctual (un-conditioned) response. Next a bell was rung at the same time as the meat was brought, until eventually the dog salivated on simply hearing the dinner bell (a "conditioned" response). Pavlov distinguished this conditioned response from such "innate" responses as a dog avoiding a flame. Thus the dog's behavior was "shaped and modified"—and this finding of classical conditioning would give rise to a century of human learning viewed as behavior modification and conditioning. Behavioral studies would be contributed by Watson (1913) and Skinner (1938 and 1954). The "conditioning" aspect of classical behaviorist training carries right down through Robert Gagne's *Conditions of Learning* (1965).

1904   The term "industrial psychology" appears for the first time, in an article.

1913   Hugo Munsterberg, father of industrial psychology, publishes *Psychology and Industrial Efficiency*. Munsterberg, a German teaching at Harvard, takes psychology out of Wundt's lab and into the street, launching "applied psychology (applied to everyday human life instead of merely lab rats). He also launches industrial-organizational psychology (I/O psychology, the psychology of the workplace), which subsequently sparks

> In 1916 Hugo Munsterberg publishes the first psychological study of the new medium of film—from the standpoint of the viewer—thereby inventing the new field of viewer or user psychology.

the *Journal of Applied Psychology* in 1917 and cadres of Ph.D.s in industrial psychology in the 1920s. Urging a powerful blend of cognitive and behaviorist (mind-body) psychology, Munsterberg studies the attitudes towards work of Boston streetcar drivers as well as of factory workers in the nascent telephone industry. Urging managers to be concerned with everyday workplace "questions of mind such as monotony, interest, and work satisfaction," he analyzes everyday tasks on the job with reference to "the mental qualities behind them," pointing ahead to what we today call "job satisfaction."

1913   John Watson officially founds academic American behaviorism with his manifesto "Psychology As the Behaviorist Views It." Rejecting the subjective introspection of a William James and other psychologists, Watson prides himself on his objective "scientific" view (modeled on nineteenth-century science), accepting only what could be "observed and measured." For Watson, internal activities such as thinking, remembering, and feeling do not exist for the scientific observer. Watson's opening remarks are programmatic for the entire movement: "Psychology as the behaviorist views it is a purely objective experimental branch of natural science. Its theoretical goal is the prediction and control of behavior. Introspection forms no part of its

> Behaviorism rejects introspection and consciousness.

methods nor does interpretation in terms of consciousness." (Freud's studies of mental illness, with their mental ramifications and stress on introspection, was obviously an entirely different movement in psychology at the time, one that, in the eyes of the behaviorists, was entirely "unscientific.")

1919   John Watson: *Psychology from the Standpoint of a Behaviorist*. Building on Thorndike, Watson creates the first textbook to extend behaviorism beyond rats to human beings. Despite inroads by Freud and the Gestaltists during the 1920s and 1930s, behaviorism will reign supreme for much of the twentieth century, particularly in training and development. The third member of the behaviorist triumvirate (along with Thorndike and Watson) was Skinner (see Fastpaths 1938 and 1953). Watson believed that we are born with only three instincts (fear, rage, and love) and that all the rest of our activities are based solely on habit, which can be "conditioned"—shaped, trained, modified, and developed—by behavioral psychologists through reinforcement.

1932   Morris Viteles publishes *Industrial Psychology*, the first book to carry this concept in its title.

1938   B. F. Skinner publishes *The Behavior of Organisms*. Helps further promote behaviorism in the United States, laying foundations for later transference from animals to the human domain. Where Pavlov had studied dogs answering dinner bells, U.S. behaviorists tended to study rats navigating mazes. Learning was connected to the rat's ability to "associate" learning maze-pathways with getting food. Centuries earlier the English philosopher John Locke had erected a theory of learning through "association" in human beings, but his writings from the early 1700s were largely ignored by educational psychologists. Skinner's views would strongly influence the world of training, including Robert Gagne.

1948 Ernest Hilgard: *Theories of Learning.* A clearly written summary of the two central trends of early twentieth century psychology: Behaviorism (association theory of Skinner) and Gestalt (which focuses on patterns or habits of present experience in order to change them, as in the field theory of Kurt Lewin).

1948 B. F. Skinner: *Walden Two.* Skinner describes how the principles of conditioning might be applied to create an ideal planned society.

1953 B. F. Skinner's *Science and Human Behavior.* Skinner turns from his 1938 work on organisms (a.k.a. rats) to take a look at human beings. Skinner's work will be introduced into the training and development world by the "Four Horsemen of Behaviorist Training," namely Gilbert, Harless, Mager, and Rummler. Skinner's programmed instruction, much like modern Web-based training, advises chunking learning into bite-sized "frames" and giving immediate feedback that reinforces the action.

1954 Skinner's article "The Science of Learning and the

Operant Conditioning: Reinforcing Results, Not Worrying About Causes

In 1938 Skinner promotes a new concept in behaviorism, which he calls "operant" conditioning. When Pavlov's dog responded to the ringing of a Russian dinner bell by salivating, it was part of a "classical" conditioning program where the learning event had been triggered by a specific stimulus—the ringing of a dinner bell. In the world of human learning, however (although Skinner still used pigeons for his experiments), things are much more complex, and it is not always possible to discern which stimulus triggers a response. Consequently Skinner introduces the bridging word "operant," meaning "influencing the operation," and thus shifts the researcher's focus from the cause of the action (stimulus) to the effect (response). Operant conditioning reinforces the operational results by means of rewards and incentives rather than trying to root out the "original cause" or "stimulus" for the action.

To take an example, let us ask the question of why you are reading this paragraph right now. The answers are probably multiple—in fact, if you look backwards in time you can no doubt come up with an endless series of connecting reasons or stimuli. Since it would be hopeless to start "reproducing"

(continued)

Art of Teaching" appears in the *Harvard Educational Review*. The article is a report from the front lines on the first teaching machines of the 1950s, which were implementing programmed instruction and were early forerunners of today's Web-based training. A teaching machine is a box about the size of a small record player. On the top surface is a window through which a question or problem can be seen on a moving paper tape underneath. The learner answers the questions by moving a slider and then turning a knob ("as simple as adjusting a knob on your television set"). If the answer is correct, the knob moves forward freely (and can "ring a bell to provide a conditioned reinforcement"). If wrong; the knob won't turn and the student has to re-set the sliders to the correct answer. A counter keeps a running tally of all answers for purposes of scoring. Unlike flash cards, "the teaching machine reports wrong answers without giving away the right answer," and the student can't proceed until the correct answer is given; hence the mastery learning involved.

these multiple stimuli to get you to repeat the action, Skinner would completely ignore the "why" questions and concentrate instead on the "shaping" or "reinforcing" of the response—reading this particular paragraph in an encyclopedia. He would simply *reward* you for having done it, rather than trying to initiate it, and encourage you with rewards, such as patting you on the back, giving you three gold stars, telling you how intelligent you are, or saying that you're going to get a promotion. This is "operant" conditioning, or "behavior modification"—reinforcing and rewarding a specific action or behavior.

1957   Skinner's *Verbal Behavior*, which still maintains a heavily behaviorist agenda.

1958   Skinner's article "Teaching Machines" appears in *Science* magazine.

1964   Skinner's article "Reflections on a Decade of Teaching Machines," appears in *Teachers College Record*. Lucid summary of his views on machine-enabled learning, plus an interesting attempt to broaden behaviorism's domain to include many aspects of its rival, cognitivism.

1984   Karen Pryor: *Don't Shoot the Dog*. A light-hearted but instructive study of behaviorism.

1985   John O'Donnell: *The Origins of Behaviorism: American Psychology 1870–1920*.

Blended Learning

Blended Learning generally refers to the combination of classroom with electronic learning. A typical example would be a classroom training that places various pre-work, home-work, tests, and follow-on sustainment activities on the Web. The idea, a good one, is that the trainer can "offload" what is more efficiently carried out at a computer screen rather than in a classroom. A proper "blend" maximizes both media (classroom and computer) for what they are best suited.

Blended learning can also refer to the combination of videotaped lectures or live Webcasts with online tests, or of personal coaching sessions with a Web course. There are endless variations. The key concept is to leverage each medium for what it does best in order to deliver the biggest payback in ROI.

> **Blended Learning Sparks a Knowledge Renaissance**
>
> In A.D. 750, the Arabs, importing and improving a technology from China, created "paper-enabled" learning (as we might call it today). By substituting inexpensive paper for expensive animal-skin vellum and parchment, the Arabs created the *paper-based manuscript*, a mass-media platform that—combined with the oral tradition of ancient Greek learning—helped ignite an explosion of learning that would lead to the Arab renaissance (800–1100) as well as to the subsequent Italian Renaissance (1400–1600).

It should be added that world-class learning has always been "blended" learning. The very first classrooms of ancient Greece were "blended" learning combinations of traditional Socratic classroom discussion (oral medium) with the new hi-tech medium of the scroll (print medium).

Cognitivism

I think, therefore I am.

—Descartes, 1630

The battle cry of the cognitive revolution is "Mind is back! A great new science of mind is born."

—B. F. Skinner, 1989

Cognitivism (from Latin, "to think") is a twentieth-century movement in psychology away from behaviorism's scientific experiments with habits, reflexes, and conditioning, and toward the study of such subjective mental states and processes as thinking, problem solving, and decision making. Cognitivism asserts that behaviorism is often overly mechanistic and simplistic when applied to the complexity of human beings, and that it tends to treat only surface symptoms and not the real problems.

In the 1960s, cognitivism, by bringing the "head" into the discussion, expands the reach of general psychology; during the 1970s it receives an added boost from the new and related fields of artificial intelligence and computer science. In the 1980s it receives yet more support from cognitive science and neuroscience. By breaking behaviorism's taboo against studying higher mental processes, cognitivism seeks to move beyond mechanistic "chains" of physical movement, and view the human mind as an information processing system. All of these related disciplines study the brain as a model of an intricately ordered communication system.

By the 1990s, cognitivism is making itself felt in departments of training as well. The new dimension that it brings to performance is vitally needed for the more complex mental tasks that are demanded by the information age. For cognitivism's effect on training design, see the books by Merrienboer and Clark in the Fastpath section below.

The chart on the following page summarizes the major differences between behaviorism and cognitivism.

FASTPATHS

1924   Jean Piaget (1896–1980): *Judgment and Reasoning in the Child.*

1956   The official launch of cognitivism (cognitive science) at a conference at MIT in Boston.

> Reporter: Don't you *know* anything?
> Yogi Berra: I don't even suspect anything.

1956   George Miller: "The Magical Number Seven, Plus or Minus Two: Some Limits on Our Capacity for Processing Information," in *The Psychological Review,* vol. 63. The classic paper that helped spark the cognitive revolution. Discusses, among other fascinating topics, why our brains can easily remember phone numbers of seven digits, but have trou-

Behaviorism (1920s–)	Cognitivism (1970s–)
Doing	Thinking
Physical tasks	Mental tasks
Lower level physical jobs	Higher level management jobs
Shapes physical habits	Teaches thinking, decision making, problem solving
Tools: punishments and rewards	Tools: creative challenges, problems to solve
Example: "cures fear of selling"	Example: "teaches you how to sell"

Backgrounds:

Pioneers: Pavlov, Watson, and Skinner, studying animals	Pioneers: Piaget and Bruner, studying children
"Objective" psychological truth	"Subjective" psychological truth
Scientific model: nineteenth-century scientism	Scientific model: twentieth-century information processing
Related to: physiological psychology	Related to: cognitive science, neuroscience

ble remembering area codes (digits 8 to 10)—something that behaviorists never worried about.

1958 Donald Broadbent: *Perception and Communication.* First book devoted to what will be called "cognitive science," the processing of information by the human mind. Views memories as storage systems, and human attention as an information filter.

1960 Jerome Bruner: *The Process of Education.* Bruner, following in Piaget's footsteps, emphasizes that cognitive (mind-based) psychology deserves equal footing with behaviorist (body-based) psychology.

> The two most powerful agencies in man's nature are reason *and mind.*
> —Plutarch: *On Education,* Greek philosopher, A.D. 100

1965 Charles Kepner and Benjamin Tregoe: *The Rational Manager: A System-*

atic Approach to Problem Solving and Decision Making. Classic performance improvement model built on cognitive problem-solving strategies.

1970s The founding of two major journals, the *Cognitive Science Journal* and *Cognitive Science Society.*

1972 Howard Gardner: *The Quest for Mind: Piaget, Levi-Strauss, and the Structuralist Movement.* Gardner, a student of Bruner's, provides a readable summary of Piaget, a cognitive child psychologist.

1979 The Cognitive Science Society is formed.

1983 Donald Schon: *The Reflective Practitioner: How Professionals Think in Action.* A brilliant book, rich in insights.

1985 Howard Gardner: *The Mind's New Science: A History of the Cognitive Revolution.* Still the best and most readable summary of cognitivism available.

1987 Donald Schon: *Educating the Reflective Practitioner: Toward a New Design for Teaching and Learning in the Professions.* A book on the same high level as Schon's previous book (1983).

1988 P. N. Johnson-Laird: *The Computer and the Mind: An Introduction to Cognitive Science.*

1989 Roger Penrose: *The Emperor's New Mind: Concerning Computers, Minds, and the Laws of Physics.* Witty, amusing, and contentious by turns, attacks the cog-sci crowd (the emperors wearing no clothes), stating that the brain is more than a collection of tiny wires and switches. A highly intelligent, important theoretical book.

1989 B. F. Skinner's "The Origins of Cognitive Thought," published in *Recent Issues in the Analysis of Behavior.* Skinner fights a rear-guard action against

---

A Cognitive Contrarian: The Zen Way to High Performance

In 1974 Timothy Gallwey writes *The Inner Game of Tennis.* Using an anticognitive approach similar to that of Zen and the martial arts, Gallwey prescribes techniques for short-circuiting cognitive feedback and bypassing the noise in our heads in order to deliver higher performance. Gallwey's approach could be called that of the "nonreflective" practitioner: "Don't think, watch the seams on the ball" is his rallying cry.

My head is like a fishbowl. Everyone sees inside it.

—Peter Lorre, German movie star, 1928

the advancing cognitivists, still insisting that cognitive processes are actually anchored in behaviorist processes.

1997   Jeroen van Merriënboer: *Training Complex Cognitive Skills*. An excellent, clearly written book from the Netherlands. Merriënboer divides the analysis and design phases of ADDIE into the sub-phases of decomposition and sequencing. Useful for designing courses for inventory management, aircraft control, policy analysis, troubleshooting manufacturing plants—any topic with heavily cognitive material in it.

> Doctor: "They'll restructure your brain."
> Woody Allen: "Nobody touches my brain!"
> —*Sleeper*, 1973

1998   Ruth Clark: *Building Expertise: Cognitive Methods for Training and Performance Improvement*. Provides a readable summary and introduction to the field.

See also
Behaviorism
Constructivism

Competencies

A man may be competent in one branch of knowledge without being competent in all.
—Aristotle, 350 B.C.

He has the competence to deal with the whole universe.
—Cervantes, *Don Quixote*, 1600

There are currently over 500 books in print featuring the word "competency" in their title. There are books on competency-based training, competency-based pay, competency-based training delivery, competency-based recruitment, competency-driven performance improvement, competency-based instruction, competency-based athletic training, and competency-based social work. In each case practitioners promise to help achieve strategic objectives through competencies, which are billed as a break-through concept in performance criteria. Competencies are definitely popular; the only problem is that almost everyone has a different notion of what a competency is.

Definition: Traits of High Performers

Competency-modeling is, quite simply, an attempt to describe work and jobs in a broader, more comprehensive way.

—Ron Zemke, 1999

Competencies are *descriptions of desired performance traits in employees.* The goal of competencies is to build a common set of standards (criteria) to improve the selection, development, and evaluation of employees. Described variously as competency maps, models, or profiles, these character traits act as criteria for performance measurement in annual reviews and promotions. As predictors of personal and organizational success, competencies can be extremely useful to human resource departments in the interviewing and hiring process, as well as in the areas of developing, appraising, promoting, and ultimately compensating employees. They are also extremely useful for self-assessment.

One example of a performance trait is independent judgment. A definition of this competency would be: *"uses discretion in interpreting company procedures to make decisions in ambiguous situations."* Other examples of performance traits are initiative, self-discipline, leadership, systems thinking, problem solving, customer focus, strategic thinking, teamwork, and empathy.

The Hierarchy of Performance Descriptors: Goals, Competencies, and Skills

As concise descriptions of a desired performance standard, competencies are more specific than goals and less specific than skills. A competency of "communicating," for instance, might include "listening" as one of its several skills. Thus *competencies represent groups or clusters of skills,* as in the following example where "leadership" is the goal:

Goal: Leadership
> *Competency*: Interpersonal Communication

> *Skill*: Listening
>> *Performance Objective* (behavioral description): "When listening, employee periodically confirms her understanding of what the speaker is saying."

Note that this is a loosely formulated performance objective, which is often used in these cases. A rigorously framed performance objective would stipulate the frequency and the conditions under which this would occur. (See Objectives: Knowledge, Skills, and Attitude.)

Origin of Competencies: Performance Objectives

The competency concept may be the most exciting and potentially promising idea to hit the training field since behavioral objectives.
—Ron Zemke, 1982

Competencies represent clusters of skills, and as such grew naturally out of early work on performance objectives (descriptions of performance that you want learners to exhibit at the end of a course, before you consider them "competent"). In the 1950s Benjamin Bloom had mapped out the classic triad of domains for objectives, namely knowledge, skills, and attitude, and in the 1960s Robert Mager contributed his path-breaking work on writing performance objectives. In the early 1970s David McClelland, a Harvard psychologist who founded the McBer consulting group, began to experiment with competencies, a level of performance-expectation that was broader than, but included, objectives.

In a seminal paper, McClelland proposed that competencies such as initiative, self-discipline, and empathy were far better predictors of high performance on the job than were the traditional IQ test. McClelland defined competencies as traits that led to superior job performance and thereby contributed to the financial success of the organization. He established these competencies by interviewing high and low performers regarding "critical events" (key behaviors) on the job. Competencies differentiated the star performer from routine performers, and were, McClelland stated, predictive of success.

Competencies: Innate or Learned?

When formulating competencies, it is necessary to distinguish between innate and learned competencies. For example, if using competencies to hire and train a sales force, one competency to look for might be "influencing for results." This competency would consist of several skills, two of which would be such learned skills as product knowledge and presentation skills. But it might also include the attribute or attitude of being an "aggressive" sales person—which is more an inborn than a learned trait. To implement the competency of "influencing for results," in other words (in a simplified example), HR will have to hire an "aggressive" sales person (an inborn trait) who will then be trained in both product knowledge and presentation skills (learned traits). The following hierarchy of performance descriptors shows what this looks like:

> *Goal*: Increased Sales
>> *Competency*: Influencing for Results
>>> *Skills, Knowledge, and Attitudes*:
>>>> Presentation skills (physical/behavioral): Learned
>>>> Product knowledge (mental/cognitive): Learned
>>>> Aggressiveness (emotional attribute): Innate

When developing competencies and their subsets of skills, knowledge, and attitudes, be sure to distinguish among traits to hire for and traits to train for. Generic off-the-shelf competency descriptions may well suffice for the former, but for the latter, organizations will have to write their own competency models.

Levels of Expertise: Abstract Traits vs. Specific Tasks

Competencies are often arranged according to organizational job levels—such as executive, manager, supervisor, and individual contributor level. Whereas on the managerial level a competency is more abstract ("being a leader"), lower level competencies can actually be akin to tasks ("answers the phone appropriately"). The following example, using the situation of a sales force, should make this clearer:

Competency: Relationship Building (for sales force)

General description of the competency: Understands client's situation, speaks their language, acknowledges their viewpoint, and helps them understand the value of the product, thereby establishing credibility and trust with the client.

Specific Levels of Expertise Under this Competency:

Job Level 1: Responds to client phone calls in a timely fashion (task-level, administrative).

Job Level 2: Manages client expectations ahead of time if there is a particular constraint associated with the product (tactical level).

Job Level 3: Creates a true partnership with the client in terms of coming up with an appropriate solution to the problem (managerial level job, a more abstract capability).

Danger of Competencies

Competencies are Humpty Dumpty words meaning only what the definer wants them to mean.

—Ron Zemke, 1982

If the power of competencies lies in their ability to focus organizations on specific performance traits as keys to organizational success, their danger is equally great: If framed too broadly, they are impossible to implement. HR departments can spend endless corporate time and money describing competencies and the performance objectives on which they are based—and not implement them properly. Every company needs to be aware of this and allocate money for implementing, as well as formulating, key competencies.

FASTPATHS

1956   Benjamin Bloom: *Taxonomy of Educational Objectives*. Bloom was the pioneer in staking out a claim for the three domains of "knowledge, skills, and attitude" in the terrain of behavioral objectives. Learning objectives are precursors and building blocks of competencies.

1962   Robert Mager: *Preparing Objectives for Programmed Instruction* (later: *Preparing Instructional Objectives*). Mager writes the classic text on how to develop and write objectives for specific skills. Mager's method is sometimes referred to as criterion-referenced instruction (CRI) because each objective sets a criterion (standard) for performance.

1973   David McClelland: "Testing for Competence Rather Than for Intelligence," *American Psychologist* 28 (1973): 14–31. A seminal paper on competencies. McClelland isolates critical personality traits in top performers.

1978   Tom Gilbert: *Human Competence: Engineering Worthy Performance.* A book more on general competence than on "competencies" as a discipline. A key text in the human performance technology (HPT) movement.

1982   Richard Boyatzis: *The Competent Manager: A Model for Effective Performance.* A classic study of competencies among managers, supervisors, and executives.

1982   William Blank: *Handbook for Developing Competency-Based Training Programs.*

1982   Ron Zemke: "Job Competencies: Can They Help You Design Better Training?" *Training* (May 1982). Zemke issues a warning about an overall lack of agreement in defining competencies, but points out their great promise.

1983   Howard Gardner: *Frames of Mind: The Theory of Multiple Intelligences.* Gardner breaks out "standardized" intelligence tests into "spatial, musical, logical, linguistic" and other more specific domains of intelligence. (See Multiple Intelligences.)

1984   David Kolb: *Experiential Learning: Experience as the Source of Learning and Development.*

1986   Robert Sternberg and R. Wagner: *Practical Intelligence: Nature and Origins of Competence in the Everyday World.*

1990   Gary Hamel and C. K. Prahalad: "The Core Competence of the Corporation," *Harvard Business Review*, May/June 1990.

1992   William Rothwell: *Mastering the Instructional Design Process* (section on "competency assessment").

1993   David Dubois: *Competency-Based Performance Improvement: A Strategy for Organizational Change.*

1993   Lyle Spencer and Signe Spencer: *Competence at Work: Models for Superior Performance.*

1998   Daniel Goleman: *Working with Emotional Intelligence.* Goleman's first chapter "Beyond Expertise" discusses competencies. Goleman relies heavily on McClelland (1973).

1998   David McClelland: "Identifying Competencies with Behavioral-Event Interviews," *Psychological Science* 9 (1998): 331–339. (See also Fastpaths 1973, McClelland.)

1999   Paul Green: *Building Robust Competencies: Linking Human Resource Systems to Organizational Strategies.*

1999   Ron Zemke: "Putting Competencies to Work," *Training* (January 1999). In a sequel to his 1982 article, Zemke issues a second warning: The time has come for HR departments who have been painstakingly compiling competency models for years "to prove themselves" through real-world implementations.

2000   William Rothwell, et al.: *The Complete Guide to Training Delivery: A Competency-Based Approach.*

2000   Kenneth Cooper: *Effective Competency Modeling and Reporting.*

See also
Learning Style
Multiple Intelligences

Constructivism

You have something within you, Theaetetus, that you're bringing forth.
—Socrates: *Theaetetus,* 450 B.C.

Education is the growth of capacities with which human beings are endowed at birth.
—Rousseau, 1762

Experiential Knowledge: Learning Through Doing and Constructing

Constructivism is less a specific technique for designing and implementing instruction than a philosophy of learning. Based on the theories of Rousseau, Dewey, and Piaget, in addition to the progressive education of the 1930s, constructivism states that students learn by doing and experience, and that they should be "guided, not taught." As Rousseau warned conventional teachers, "You think you are teaching the student what the world is like; he is only learning the maps." As Dewey, Rousseau's pupil, stressed, "Avoid repeating formulas, and substitute the process of personal discovery." Where traditional lecture-based "instructivism" stresses the role of the teacher, constructivism stresses the role of the student, and states that we learn best through constructing our own mental models (schemas). We then check out how these schemas stack up against reality, and make our decisions accordingly. Knowledge is constructed through interacting with our environment.

Constructivism enjoys a long intellectual heritage. Because it focuses on an individualist problem-solving method, it overlaps with both guided experiential learning and discovery learning. Constructivism is grounded in the psychological "inward turn" of Kantian philosophy in 1800, which in turn gave rise to German phenomenology in the early 1900s. In the 1950s the movement arrived at the door of American educational institutions through the work of the Swiss child psychologist Jean Piaget. Piaget asserted that children learn, not from being handed information, but from direct experience with life and a constant unconscious testing of their mental models (*schemas*, in the words of the phenomenologists) against the world. Piaget described the learning process as one of "assimilation and accommodation." We assimilate present learning experiences into past structures (in our heads), but at the same time subtly accommodate (shift) those same mental structures to accommodate the new experience. We thereby constantly "construct" our vision of the world (which is the position of the phenomenologist philosophers). The Russian psychologist Lev Vygotsky had already expressed similar thoughts in 1934 in his *Thinking and Speaking*, although he focused more on the social context of learning.

> Instead of rote memorization, use the sure process of personal discovery.
> —John Dewey, *Schools of Tomorrow*, 1915

Curriculum as Scaffold or Environment

Give the students an environment which is full of interesting things that need to be done.

—John Dewey, *Schools of Tomorrow*, 1915

Perhaps because of the connection with Piaget, constructivism has had less influence on adult learning than on the kindergarten-through-twelfth-grade curriculum, particularly its math and science branches. Because of its methodology of guided exploratory learning, constructivism speaks of designing "scaffolds" or "authentic environments" rather than designing "courses," and it refers to teachers as "coaches and facilitators." Only the experiential acquisition of knowledge really counts.

In conclusion, constructivism is easy to theorize about, but sometimes difficult and expensive to implement due to the high level of interactivity involved. However—like all experiential learning—given the appropriate budget, adequate learner-time, and the right situation, it can be extremely effective.

The teacher, if he is wise, leads you to the threshold of your own mind.
—Kahlil Gibran, Lebanese Mystic, 1920

FASTPATHS

1915   John Dewey: *The Schools of Tomorrow.* The importance of Rousseau for progressive education (as well as later constructivism).

1924   Jean Piaget (1896–1980) *Judgment and Reasoning in the Child.*

1934   Lev Vygotsky (1896–1934) publishes *Thinking and Speaking.* Soviet psychologist who develops a genetic approach to human learning, anticipating much of Jean Piaget's genetic epistemology of the 1950s. Published by MIT in translation in 1962 as *Thought and Language.*

1950   Jean Piaget: *Introduction to Genetic Epistemology.* Piaget studies the development (genesis) of knowledge (epistemology) in children and youth.

1954   Jean Piaget: *The Child's Construction of Reality.* Drawing on German phenomenology (theory of perception), the Swiss psychologist proposes a developmental view of humans and learning. He distinguishes four phases in the mental development of children:

   1. sensory motor coordination (up to age 2)
   2. intuitive (the labeling or naming of objects, ages 2 to 7)
   3. concrete (the classifying of objects, ages 7 to 12)
   4. abstract (cognitively thinking-about-things, symbolical reasoning, ages 12 to 16)

1960   Jerome Bruner: *The Process of Education.* Building on Piaget, Bruner helps launch the constructivist movement in the United States. Content is largely focused on science and math learning for young children.

1963   John Flavell: *The Developmental Psychology of Jean Piaget.* Good summary of Piaget's psychological work.

1966   Peter Berger and Thomas Luckman: *The Social Construction of Reality: A Treatise in the Sociology of Knowledge.* Heavily theoretical.

1969   R. Beard: *An Outline of Piaget's Developmental Psychology.* Provides useful description of Piaget's major theories and their implications for teachers.

1978   Lev Vygotsky (translation of earlier work): *Mind in Society: The Development of Higher Psychological Processes.*

1981   Howard Gardner: *The Quest for Mind: Piaget, Levi-Strauss, and the Struc-turalist Movement.* Excellent summary of cognitivism (to which constructivism is related because of its belief in mental models).

1983   Philip Johnson-Laird: *Mental Models: Towards a Cognitive Science of Language, Inference, and Consciousness.* Excellent on individual mindset "schemas" (as opposed to group mindset "paradigms").

1985   Kenneth Gergen (ed.): *The Social Construction of the Person.* Sociological view.

1995   John Searle: *The Construction of Social Reality.* Philosophical view.

1995   B. G. Wilson (ed.): *Designing Constructivist Learning Environments.* Good anthology.

1995   L. Steffe and J. Gale (eds.): *Constructivism in Education.* Includes important piece by Paul Ernest, "The One and the Many," on the many conflicting definitions and schools of constructivism.

1996   Yasmin Kafai and M. Resnick (eds.): *Constructionism in Practice: Designing, Thinking, and Learning in a Digital World.*

1996   Brent Wilson (ed.): *Constructivist Learning Environments.* Includes useful articles on instructional design.

1999   Ian Hacking: *The Social Construction of What?* A refreshingly open-eyed review of the many fields that "constructivism" has influenced, including that of cognitive psychology.

See also
Rousseau
Dewey

Distance Learning

From Snail Mail to Webcast

Distance learning or distance education is a broad term designating, as one might expect, any learning-at-a-distance. As such it encompasses a vast array of transmission devices; e-mail, snail mail, telephone,

St. Paul's Epistles: Early Distance Learning

Ancient precursors of distance learning were those Greek runners who carried scrolls from Rome to Athens. And in the New Testament, Paul's letter to the Corinthians was carried by a runner from Rome to Greece, and represented early distance learning for the Corinthians.

satellite, radio, mailed videotapes, audio-cassettes, television, video-conferencing, e-learning, and live Webcasts could all be included as "distance learning" modes.

From Correspondence School to E-Learning

The day is coming when the work done by correspondence will be greater than that done in the classroom.
—William Rainey Harper, 1885 (father of the junior college movement)

Distance learning originated in vocational correspondence schools that flourished during the heyday of industrialism in the mid-1800s and served to educate the working classes and women. An enormous range of topics was taught by mail, ranging from shorthand and drafting to home economics. A full century later, in the 1960s, the British "open learning" movement and its "university without walls" were conceived in the same spirit, and by 2000, e-learning or Web-based training continued the tradition.

FASTPATHS

1997   Karen Mantyla and J. Gividen: *Distance Learning: A Step-by-Step Guide for Trainers.*

1998   Alan Chute et al. (eds.): *The McGraw-Hill Handbook of Distance Learning.*

2000   Nancy Stevenson: *Distance Learning for Dummies.*

> **See also**
> Adult Learning

E-Learning

E-learning, or electronic-learning, is training carried over the World Wide Web. It can also mean training carried over an intranet inside a company. Because Web content is digital in nature, a large array of pre-built training—ranging from Webcasts, CD-ROM, and CBT to streaming media—are all grist for e-learning's mill.

The two great advantages of e-learning are that (1) its content can be centrally updated (on a server), and (2) it can track learners' activities (in a database). In practical terms this means the realization of a host of dreams that have been harbored by trainers for years, but that could never be realized in a pre-Web world. These include: Level 3 evaluation (noting whether training transferred to the job), Level 4 evaluation (did the training carry a financial payback), and tracking student progress through a curriculum (classroom, online, or self-study) by means of a dynamic transcript. Such transcripts can log not only classes attended and self-studies completed, but can also track scores on tests and certifications, and any informal learning, coaching, or mentoring sessions that have been recorded as well. E-learning does not replace classrooms or self-studies, but augments these, "blending" them with what the Web does best: providing online pretests and post-tests, information lookups, post-course refreshers, and collaborative learning communities. However, just as with any delivery medium, e-learning must be constructed around sound instructional design principles, and tied into business objectives.

Prediction: The Medium Will Disappear

"The medium is the message" is the slogan of any new technology on the rise, loudly and boisterously hyping itself. When it has matured, however, the medium disappears into the background, and the message shifts to center stage. We no longer speak of "book" learning, for instance. And thus in the course of time, e-learning will also shed its "e" and become just plain "learning." At that point, we will know that e-learning has grown up.

> **Synchronous vs. Asynchronous Courses**
>
> *Synchronous* courses are live Webcasts (Latin and Greek: *syn-chronos*: "in simultaneous time").
> *Asynchronous* courses are recorded Webcasts or regular courses (Latin and Greek: *a-synchronos*: "out of time").

FASTPATHS

1997   Brandon Hall: *The Web-Based Training Cookbook.*

2001   Roger Schank: *Designing World-Class E-Learning.*

2001   Marc Rosenberg: *E-Learning: Strategies for Delivering Knowledge in the Digital Age.*

2002   Allison Rossett (ed.): *ASTD E-Learning Handbook: Best Practices, Strategies, and Case Studies for an Emerging Field.*

2002   Ruth Clark and Richard Mayer: *E-Learning and the Science of Instruction.*
2003   George Piskurich (ed.): *The AMA Handbook of E-Learning.*

See also
Electronic Performance Support Systems (EPSS)
Extreme Learning Systems
The Web Model: Dimension 7

Electronic Performance Support Systems

An electronic performance support system (EPSS) generally refers to an online help system, or electronic job aid. Providing context-sensitive help-on-demand, EPSS is integrated with many computer applications. In some cases the help (performance support) is personified through an expert advisor or online wizard, and in this sense is similar to the so-called expert systems of artificial intelligence. EPSS is now generally referred to in the short form of "performance support." It is often a subset or feature of knowledge management systems.

FASTPATHS

1989   AT&T launches the first EPSS system, an online help system to support employees in outlining and writing tests.

1991   Gloria Gery: *Electronic Performance Support Systems.* Gery's text helped found the "online help" movement of the 1990s. Gery's book describes case studies of EPSS systems.

See also
Job Aids
Knowledge Management

Emotional Intelligence

Anyone can become angry—that's easy. But to be angry with the right person, to the right degree, at the right time, for the right purpose, and in the right way—that's not easy.

—Aristotle, *The Nicomachean Ethics,* 350 B.C.

Emotional intelligence, according to Daniel Goleman, is the learned capability of managing feelings and emotional relationships in order to produce outstanding performance. According to Goleman, emotional intelligence predicts success better than any traditional IQ test. The roots of emotional intelligence lie with Howard Gardner, who in 1983 expanded the traditional dual-aptitude test (math and verbal) into a system of seven intelligences. In 1990, inspired by Gardner, Peter Salovey and John Mayer proposed that there was an eighth intelligence, namely emotional intelligence. In 1995 Daniel Goleman, an ex-*New York Times* reporter specializing in psychological topics, spread the word with his best-seller, *Emotional Intelligence: Why It Can Matter More Than IQ*. Goleman was essentially reviving the standard triadic psychological model of knowledge (cognitive domain), skills (physical domain), and feelings (emotional or affective domain), and focusing on the third—the domain of the emotions. Goleman, together with two other researchers, followed up in 2002 with *Primal Leadership: Realizing the Power of Emotional Intelligence*. What follows is a brief summary of Goleman's major categories.

Emotional Intelligence: Five Domains

Goleman, basing his definition of emotional intelligence (EI) on Salovey and Mayer (see Fastpaths 1990), distinguishes five domains of emotional intelligence (see Fastpaths 1995, Goleman):

Toward oneself:

1. Knowing one's emotions
2. Motivating oneself
3. Managing one's own emotions

Toward others:

4. Recognizing emotions in others
5. Handling relationships

Each of the domains adds a crucial set of skills for resonant leadership (see Fastpaths 2002, Goleman).

Emotional Leadership: Six Styles

Successful leaders effectively handle their emotions when dealing with others, and Goleman distinguishes six leadership styles (see Fastpaths 2002, Goleman):

1. Affiliative
2. Coaching
3. Democratic
4. Visionary
5. Commanding
6. Pace-Setting

Top leaders utilize the full repertoire of styles, invoking whichever is appropriate to the given situation.

Leadership Dissonance, Leadership Resonance

In *Primal Leadership*, Goleman defines emotional intelligence in the leadership domain along the two axes of "resonance" and "dissonance." Where resonance brings out the best in people by making them feel positive about their emotions, dissonance creates groups that "feel emotionally discordant." The "ratio of resonance to dissonance," he sums up, "determines an organization's emotional climate and relates directly to how it performs" (see Fastpaths 2002).

Goleman has made an impressive beginning in mapping out the descriptive domains of EI. The next step will be to build on this foundation, producing a robust discipline based on tools such as the emotional competence inventory, and on real business situations.

FASTPATHS

1956   Benjamin Bloom: *Taxonomy of Educational Objectives: The Classification of Educational Goals*. The classic text on the three domains: knowledge, skills, and emotional abilities.

1982   Richard Boyatzis: *The Competent Manager: A Model for Effective Performance*. A study of competencies among managers, supervisors, and executives.

1983   Howard Gardner: *Frames of Mind: The Theory of Multiple Intelligences*. The breakthrough book on multiple intelligences; it proposes seven intelligences.

1990   Peter Salovey and John Mayer: "Emotional Intelligence," *Imagination, Cognition, and Personality* 9 (1990): 185–211. Salovey and Mayer outline the first model and definition of an "emotional" intelligence.

1995   Daniel Goleman: *Emotional Intelligence: Why It Can Matter More Than IQ.* Goleman's best-seller sets the agenda for the eighth intelligence, that of the emotions.

1995   Howard Gardner: *Leading Minds: An Anatomy of Leadership.* This, plus Gardner's 1983 book, is a major influence on Goleman's emotional leadership notion.

1997   Peter Salovey and David Sluyter (eds.): *Emotional Development and Emotional Intelligence.*

1998   Daniel Goleman: *Working with Emotional Intelligence.* Emotional intelligence as applied to the workplace rather than to private everyday life.

2001   Daniel Goleman et al. (eds.): *The Emotionally Intelligent Workplace.* Contains Lyle Spencer's "The Economic Value of Emotional Intelligence Competencies and EIC-Based HR Programs."

2001   Adele Lynn: *The Emotional Intelligence Activity Book.*

2002   Daniel Goleman, Richard Boyatzis, and Annie McKee: *Primal Leadership: Realizing the Power of Emotional Intelligence.* Goleman and two other researchers tie emotional intelligence to corporate leadership.

See also
Competencies
Multiple intelligences

Hawthorne Effect

The Hawthorne effect refers to the phenomenon that mere attention to employees can increase performance.

The Magic of Being Observed

During the years from 1924 through 1932 a series of experiments was conducted at Western Electric's Hawthorne Works in Cicero, Illinois. The results of the experiments, which were carried out by researchers from

Harvard, were published between 1933 and 1939 under the direction of Professor Elton Mayo, and they are often viewed as the first major call for a "human relations" management philosophy. In the experiment, researchers increased plant lighting to the level of bright cheery sunlight—and worker productivity, predictably, increased. However, when researchers dimmed plant lighting to the levels of faint moonlight, *productivity still increased!* Obviously more was going on than just changes in lighting. The major reason for increased productivity: Mere attention by the researchers (which was perceived by the workers as respect and interest in their activities) had improved their performance. In fact, only when the workers finally became used to being observed did the effect wear off and productivity level out.

This effect, now known as the Hawthorne effect, has had various interpretations, but the general consensus is the following: *Human beings perform at higher levels when they are simply being attended to respectfully by a manager.* This simple insight into human behavior still has to be properly implemented in corporations. The astounding fact is that no training, no pay increase, no interventions, no gap analysis, no tangible recognition or participative management technique was involved in the experiment. From the workers' point of view, the mere awareness of being a valued member in something larger than themselves expanded their sense of mission and thereby their ability to perform at higher levels. This larger vision, of course, is what mission statements in every corporate charter are intended to convey, but often fail to because they remain completely abstract.

The Power of Recognition by Others

Interestingly, the Hawthorne effect mirrored Dale Carnegie's discoveries at the same time. During the 1920s and 1930s Carnegie was also discovering the power of what he called "specific appreciation" of employee performance (1936). And similar phenomena were being recognized in animals by behaviorists in the 1930s in their studies of the powers of reinforcement (instead of punishment) in the shaping of animal behavior. Further recognition of the power of attention as motivation was later recorded by Whyte (1955), McGregor (1960), Vroom (1964), and Blanchard and Johnson (1981), the latter with their "one-minute praisings."

FASTPATHS

1933   Elton Mayo: *The Human Problems of an Industrial Civilization.* Mayo's reports on the "Hawthorne effect."

1936   Dale Carnegie: *How to Win Friends and Influence People.*

1945   Elton Mayo: *The Social Problems of an Industrial Civilization.*

1951   Kurt Lewin: *Field Theory in Social Science: Selected Theoretical Papers.*

1955   William F. Whyte (ed.): *Money and Motivation: An Analysis of Incentives in Industry.* To achieve optimum output one must consider motivation as well as money.

1960   Douglas McGregor: *The Human Side of Enterprise.* Initiates the "human relations" movement in management. (See Management Theory, People-Centered)

1964   Victor Vroom: *Work and Motivation.* Helps popularize Kurt Lewin's work in social psychology, organizational development, and motivation.

1981   Ken Blanchard and S. Johnson: *The One-Minute Manager.*

2001   Jay Shafritz and J. Ott (eds): *Classics of Organization Theory.*

See also
Management Theory, People-Centered

Human Factors and Ergonomics

Human factors refers to ergonomics (from Greek "work" plus "economics," meaning efficient work), the proper design of keyboards, workstations, and mice so that they are "user friendly" to eye and mind—and physically less stressful on the user's body. The design process is generally carried out through usability tests during product development.

The discipline of human factors originated in training and development efforts during World War II. Submarine navigation and weapons systems were called "man-machine systems," meaning they involved human as well as machine "factors." For example, human factors referred to how navigators operated dials, levers, dashboards, and instrument panels, and machine factors referred to how switchboards, in turn, controlled submarines, planes, and computerized anti-aircraft gunnery.

Today ergonomics is an important part of computer manufacturing as well as of the design of work stations. By extension it sometimes refers to interface design as well.

FASTPATHS

1949 Alphonse Chapanis et al.: *Applied Experimental Psychology: Human Factors in Engineering Design.*

1957 "Human Factors Society of America" founded; later renamed "Human Factors and Ergonomics Society." *See*: www.HFES.org.

1981 Wesley Woodson: *Human Factors Design Handbook.*

1987 Gavriel Salvendy (ed.): *Handbook of Human Factors and Ergonomics.*

1989 Jack Adams: *Human Factors Engineering.*

1996 Thomas O'Brien and S. Charlton (editors): *Handbook of Human Factors Testing and Evaluation.*

1997 Christopher Wickens, Sallie Gordon, and Yili Liu: *An Introduction to Human Factors Engineering.*

▬ Human Performance Technology ▬

Human performance technology (HPT) is not as forbidding as it sounds. The term refers to the "science of improving human performance," and embraces a broad systems model for improving the performance of individuals, groups, and organizations. It is practiced by the professional organization ISPI (International Society for Performance Improvement), whose model can be seen as a specific version of what is generally called "performance improvement." Originating in the behaviorism of the late 1950s, HPT originally referred to "behavioral" engineering, but has since been broadened to include cognitive (mental) dimensions as well.

For a generalized, high-level version of the model, see the section on Performance Improvement and Performance Consulting, in particular the seven factors driving organizational performance. For the latest version of the official HPT model itself, go to the ISPI Web site at www.ispi.org. The HPT methodology is perhaps best understood through its history. Here is a rapid chronology of the movement:

FASTPATHS

1962   The National Society for Programmed Instruction (NSPI) is founded, taking its name from the 1950s vogue for the teaching machines and programmed instruction of the behavioral psychologist B. F. Skinner. Later, following the trends (and employing an economy of acronym), the organization eventually becomes the International Society for Performance Improvement (ISPI).

1960s Thomas Gilbert (1927–1995), a student of Skinner's and father of the human performance movement, begins offering his first workshops in "performance improvement."

1970s Geary Rummler, a leader in the human performance improvement movement, helps design Kepner Tregoe's "performance system" consulting practice (see 1990).

1978   Tom Gilbert: *Human Competence: Engineering Worthy Performance*. This is the book resulting from Gilbert's earlier workshops in the 1960s and 1970s. Despite a difficult style, the book, which describes a behavioral-engineering model for performance improvement, has become a guiding academic work of the HPT movement. Gilbert defines performance very concretely as the "accomplishments" of a particular behavior, not the behavior itself. Workplace results are what count, not the activities that get us there. Gilbert also inaugurates gap analysis—the analysis of the "performance improvement potential" (PIP) of an individual—as the spread (or performance differential) between exemplary and average performers. Gilbert's work still stands as a powerfully pragmatic model for any performance consultant.

> "If we make people's pay contingent on their performance, tell them clearly what we expect of them (and whether they have delivered it), and give them clear instruction when they need it—they will rise to exemplary levels of performance."
> —Tom Gilbert, 1992

1990   Geary Rummler (with Alan Brache): *Improving Performance: How to Manage the White Space on the Organization Chart*. A superb systematic study of performance improvement techniques, on the three levels of organization, process, and performer/job. The book is rich in theoretical insights as well as practical examples. Rummler is one of the masters in the performance improvement movement. This is must-reading for anyone who is a performance consultant.

1992   Harold Stolovitch and Erica Keeps (eds.): *The Handbook of Human Performance Technology.* An 800-page tome by various hands, sponsored by ISPI. A veritable summa of the HPT movement, from its 1960s behaviorist roots (articles by Gilbert, Harless, and Mager) through its 1990s cognitive and performance consulting phases (Rummler and others). Difficult going for beginners, but extremely valuable for advanced practitioners. Often cited as the bible of HPT.

2002   Harold Stolovitch and Erica Keeps: *Telling Ain't Training.* A book on how and why we learn, and how to make learning stick.

2002   ISPI launches an official certification process for HPT practitioners.

> ***See also***
> Behaviorism
> Cognitivism

Informal Learning

Informal learning is learning-on-the-job, or any learning not systematized—such as mentoring and coaching. Like its ancestor in the Middle Ages—the apprenticeship—informal learning is a vital part in any training and learning program, particularly when deployed in conjunction with formal training and performance classes. Informal learning can include a wide array of activities ranging from brown bag lunches and collective learning sessions to virtual learning communities on the Web.

FASTPATHS

2000   Victoria Marsick and M. Volpe (eds.): *Advances in Developing Human Resources: Informal Learning On the Job.*

Information Mapping

Information mapping is a term used by instructional designers to refer to the proper layout of print materials or on-screen text. Formatting issues such as sidebars, running subheads, and structured writing are addressed, as well as the proper placement of illustrations and graphics. The term was coined in the 1960s by Robert Horn, who emphasized the importance of proper and consistent formatting for training binders. Today the term includes interface and screen design as well.

FASTPATHS

1969   Robert Horn: *Information Mapping for Learning and Reference.*

1983   Edward Tufte: *The Visual Display of Quantitative Information.* Tufte is one of the great graphic designers of all times. All three of his books are highly recommended.

1989   Robert Horn: *Mapping Hypertext.*

1990   Edward Tufte: *Envisioning Information.*

1997   Edward Tufte: *Visual Explanations: Images and Quantities, Evidence and Narrative.*

Intervention

An intervention (literally, an "assistance," analogous to a medical intervention) is any performance initiative that steps into an organization with the intent of improving its efficiency and effectiveness. The term is often employed by organizational developers for change management initiatives. Among the many books on organizational development and interventions, two of the pioneering ones are listed below.

FASTPATHS

1970   Chris Argyris: *Intervention Theory and Method.*

1972   Wendell French and Cecil Bell: *Organization Development: Behavioral Science Interventions for Organization Improvement.*

See also
Organizational Development

Job Aids

Job aids are checklists or memory-joggers, what the French call *aides-memoire*. A common example of a job aid is the preflight checklist used by an airline pilot. With its low cost and its solution to a potential life-and-death performance problem, it is a perfect example of the potential ROI (return on investment) for even low-tech job aids. In factories, job aids—called process sheets—display manufacturing specs. There are also electronic job aids, including electronic performance support systems (EPSS), online drop-down lists or instruction sheets, and online help. As part of a larger knowledge management system, job aids can contain mission-critical procedures to follow, and avoid costly mistakes.

Level 3 Transfer: Job Aids and On-the-Job Performance

Inside every fat course is a thin job aid crying to get out.
—Joe Harless, 1970

The most important function of job aids is to link training to practice. Job aids contain the key facts and procedures that need to be reinforced on the job. Doubt the value of job aids? Just walk down any row of cubicles and note the flowcharts, wall charts, and list of procedures on the cubicle walls. Most of these are job aids and quick reference tools, and the only living reminder of trainings delivered months earlier.

Benefits

For a small tool, a job aid provides large benefits. A job aid is:

- *Effective*—pinpoints critical procedures
- *Fast*—instant access
- *Low Cost*—more impact per dollar than any other training technology
- *Updatable*—whether hardcopy or electronic

What other performance improvement tool can match these criteria all at once? The field for job aids is endless and untapped.

FASTPATHS

1967 Albert Chalupsky and T. Kopf: *Job Performance Aids and Their Impact on Manpower Utilization.*

1970 Joe Harless: *An Ounce of Analysis Is Worth a Pound of Objectives.* Includes consideration of job aids.

1980 Claude Lineberry and D. Bullock: *Job Aids.*

1991 Allison Rossett and Jeannette Gautier-Downes: *A Handbook of Job Aids.* One of the classic texts.

1999 Saundra Williams: *Performance Support Systems and Job Aids.*

See also
Knowledge Management
Learning Objects
Electronic Performance Support Systems

Kaizen: Continuous Improvement

In 1986, Masaaki Imai introduced to the Western world the Japanese word *kaizen,* and the concept has since passed into the language of learning and performance. Literally meaning "continuous performance improvement," kaizen was originally deployed exclusively in the manufacturing sector in Japan, particularly in the automotive industry, where it referred to steady small-step improvements in quality, on-time delivery, and lowered cost.

Focusing on eliminating waste and inefficiencies in processes and systems, kaizen has since spread to soft skills and become a well-known and widely practiced management philosophy. Kaizen's start in the West was at a propitious time, for it was ushered in during the rise of TQM in the 1980s, just before the performance improvement trend began to take off in the 1990s.

Incrementalism: The Magic of Task-Specific Small-Step Transformations

Kaizen shuns the inflated rhetoric of an organizational "reinvention" or "transformation" and targets instead small quantum shifts in infrastructure. It believes in small-scale incremental improvements and piecemeal process engineering. With a practical feet-on-the-ground philosophy of organizational development, kaizen focuses on task-specific small-step improvements that fine-tune organizations through gradual and orderly advances; in place of paradigm-shattering breakthroughs, there is daily evolution. The magic is one of productive minimalism rather than extreme shifts.

Long-Term Attention to Detail: Power from Below

Similar to the practice of "lessons learned," kaizen preaches attention to detail. And as with lessons learned, kaizen is also long-term, and is typically implemented by middle management and line workers, with encouragement and direction from above. Thus, as a business strategy, it involves everyone in an organization working together, in order to make improvements without large capital investments.

In a world loud with the preaching of "global solutions," the power of kaizen lies in its continuous solving of micro-problems; it thrives in companies that nurture sustained small-step improvements.

FASTPATHS

1986   Masaaki Imai: *Kaizen: The Key to Japanese Competitive Success.*

1996   James Womack and Dan Jones: *Lean Thinking: Banish Waste and Create Wealth in Your Corporation.*

1997   Masaaki Imai: *Gemba Kaizen: A Commonsense, Low-Cost Approach to Management.*

See also
Action Learning
Performance Improvement and Performance Consulting
Total Quality Management

Knowledge Management

Knowledge management is strategic information management.
—Don Marchand and F. Horton, *Infotrends,*1986

In my profession, Watson, all sorts of odd knowledge becomes useful, and my room is a storehouse of it.
—Sherlock Holmes, *The Adventure of the Three Garridebs,* 1925

Knowledge management is the art of managing corporate memory, the craft of keeping up the company's filing cabinet. As a strategic form of information management, it represents information technology's latest gambit in its self-transformation from backroom support function to front-office strategist. Deploying enterprise-wide databases for the rapid storage and retrieval of intellectual capital, best practices, and mission-critical information, "knowledge management" captures, classifies, and indexes strategic information for use by all employees. Common everyday examples of knowledge management include staff directories on Web sites, "frequently asked questions" on tech-support Web sites (FAQs as knowledge base), and Amazon.com's pop-up lists of "related books you might be interested in."

> Knowledge management is an integrated, systematic approach to identifying, managing, and sharing an enterprise's information assets, including databases, documents, policies and procedures, as well as previously unarticulated expertise and experience held by individual workers.
> —U.S. Army Report, 1999

Convergences: Knowledge Objects and Learning Objects

At a time when HR departments are transforming themselves from bureaucratic training units into cutting-edge performance consultancies, IT departments, similarly, are shifting from sheer data-entry centers to knowledge strategists. The new roles reflect broader concerns, including a focus on company-centered performance. As training courses are being broken out into small chunks of performance support (learn-

> **Evolution of Ask-the-Expert Systems**
> - Artificial Intelligence: Expert Systems, 1980s
> - Electronic Performance Support System: Online Help, 1990s
> - Knowledge Management Systems: Knowledge Objects, 2000s

ing objects), IT departments are redesigning their databases as "knowledge management systems," and chunking them into what they call "knowledge objects." A grand commingling of HR and IT is taking place at the level of data and information. Their mutual interest is obvious: Learning objects stress reuse of content pieces within *curriculums*, knowledge objects emphasize reuse within the *organization*. As databases become knowledge bases and thus a platform for HR's courseware, both sides will benefit.

Backgrounds: Lessons Learned

Knowledge management has a long history. As early as the 1960s, AT&T's research arm, Bell Labs, had come up with a paper-based prototype for a knowledge management system (see Fastpaths 1999, Jack Gordon). Upon completion of a project, the project leader would write up the "lessons learned" and file these in a central index, a hardcopy database. Before starting a new project, the new project leader would review the database for any relevant past project reports and apply these to the new project. Personal knowledge sharing was also encouraged. In fact, line worker project leaders were encouraged to ask specialists within the company—even Nobel Prize laureates—for help. Through this company-wide knowledge sharing system, Bell Labs was able to maintain a competitive edge in research and development for decades.

Beyond Industrial Age "Warehousing, Mining, and Drilling"

I've come to the conclusion that the most concrete thing in the world is information.
                                        —Edward Fredkin, digital physicist, 1986

The very metaphors tell a story. In the beginning, IT managed data (raw facts, or literally, "what is given"). It moved in a world that still lived in the industrial age, with its metaphors of data "mining, warehousing, and drilling down." In its most recent incarnations, however, IT is decking itself out with more appropriate information-age metaphors—such as knowledge discovery, knowledge sharing, and knowledge management.

Organizational Challenges

The challenge for knowledge management will be less technological than organizational. For knowledge management requires the partnering of different departments. One typical example would be the partnering of a line unit such as sales and marketing (for content) with information technology (for deployment) and with human resources (for information design). Moreover the well-designed and well-maintained knowledge management database requires at least three experts on staff: a content expert, a database designer/programmer, and a learning designer. Such interdepartmental collaboration and cooperation will come about only if these departments leave their egos outside the meeting room door.

A Four-Step Model

Miss Lemon's private thoughts and dreams were entirely concentrated on a new filing system—which she was slowly perfecting in the recesses of her mind.

—Agatha Christie, *The Labours of Hercules,* 1947

Knowledge management generally follows a four-step process:

1. *Gather Existing Documents and Document Undocumented Knowledge.* Existing documentation could include HTML, Word, PDF, Power-Point, or Excel documents plus e-mails and attachments. It could also include white papers, industry reports, corporate libraries, and Web site links, as well as—and this is the most difficult process—the documenting of (orally circulating) best practices, procedures and processes, tips and tricks, and any competitive information.

2. *Organize Information.* This step is crucial: Here raw information is turned into "knowledge." The first step is to create an outline, taxonomy, or knowledge-map, which classifies document content into categories. This phase can become as technologically complex as one wishes, including the use of a text-search engine deployed for key-word searches (an automated "spider" crawling through all company documents and servers to retrieve information) or the utilization of taxonomy software to categorize documents. And finally, the content must be chunked and grouped and cross-indexed into a multi-level Knowledge Web.

3. *Design Interface*. An absolutely key phase, for without a user-friendly interface, the new Knowledge Web will not be used, no matter how sophisticated the relational database is.

4. *Update System on a Real-Time Basis.* In their forecasting process for knowledge management systems, organizations often overlook the sizable expense of this final step, which amounts to a permanent operating expense. Maintenance of the system involves more than a database administrator and tech support for staff. It includes additional staff who will carry out the daily capture, updating, revising, editing, formatting, re-sorting, and re-linking of the new information that will flow in, making sure this is cross-referenced to the old and ensuring that the navigation system continues to function properly with any new content categories. Content experts must be on staff to qualify the new content, and users to tag it in terms of on-the-job criticality. If compliance or standards documents are involved in the knowledge base, expensive content experts or even lawyers must be allocated to the project and process as well. As we said in the beginning, knowledge management, if more than company phone numbers and FAQs, can be an expensive business.

The Challenge of Capturing Tacit (Undocumented) Knowledge

We know more than we know we know.
                    —Michael Polanyi, *Personal Knowledge*, 1958

If a man reaches the top, he's not going to tell you how he really got there.
                    —Senior executive of large U.S. corporation
                    (from Vance Packard, *The Pyramid Climbers*, 1962)

Like any new discipline, knowledge management faces its challenges. Part of its vision, for example, is to capture and disseminate oral or "tacit" knowledge. Tacit knowledge (literally "silent" knowledge) is knowledge that has not yet been written down by the company, and which circulates orally throughout the organization. Such information is colloquially referred to in organizations as tribal knowledge, voodoo, folklore, or just old-fashioned tips and tricks. Whatever it is called, it is transmitted through the media channels of the water cooler and hallway talk, and its content can range from typical shortcuts or rules of thumb (heuristics) to innovative processes and in-house trade secrets. The assumption of knowledge management is that if all this valuable information and know-how can be written down and indexed (metatagged), a powerful new performance support system or knowledge engine will be created.

This is absolutely true. But before performance consultants launch into documenting worker shortcuts and innovations company-wide, a number of troubling questions have to be answered. First, are company employees willing to divulge their tricks of the trade for company-wide distribution on a public database? "Job security," through withholding key information, is a customary strategy in almost all organizations and professions. Not only are positions and promotions in the company at stake, but employees also fear being replaced by cheaper and/or younger labor once they have divulged all their trade secrets and these have been printed out on a mass basis as company job aids. In some assembly-line manufacturing plants where the machines are computerized, management is trying to do an end-run around this problem by setting the computerized assembly-line to automatically record each motion the workers make, so that the time-and-motion workers' best practices are automatically (and sometimes secretly) recorded in a database. Digital Big Brother is watching in some plants.

Other questions also arise. Will incentives be given to employees for capturing and writing down and exposing the silent knowledge in their heads? Will the following be a common request on company bulletin boards: "Informants Needed: Cash Reward for Information Captured Alive"? Will a new department be created to capture, index, and manage the new influx of "silent" data? Who will track and award the bonuses for contributing to the knowledge base? Will employees be given some sort of guarantee that they will not be laid off if they divulge trade secrets? How would this work? Such questions as these need to be addressed if knowledge management is to become a force in the twenty-first century and avoid the pitfalls of earlier techno-utopian ventures. Artificial intelligence's "expert systems" of the 1980s, for instance, were much over-hyped, and notoriously failed at delivering.

The following Fastpaths titles are intended as tools to bring knowledge management down to the level of corporate reality and make it a success.

FASTPATHS

He had a horror of destroying documents, especially those which were connected with his past cases, and yet it was only once every year or two that he could muster the energy to docket and arrange them.
—Sherlock Holmes, *The Musgrave Ritual*, 1893

1949   Claude Shannon and Warren Weaver: *The Mathematical Theory of Communication*. The revolutionary book that ushered in our awareness of "the information age," a work in which the authors, engineers at AT&T's Bell Laboratories, defined information as "energy."

1958   Michael Polanyi: *Personal Knowledge*. The book that inaugurates the discussion of "tacit" knowledge.

1962   Fritz Machlup: *The Production and Distribution of Knowledge in the United States*. First major attempt to describe the emerging "knowledge" worker as opposed to the "industrial" worker. First definition of the "knowledge" industry.

1966   Michael Polanyi: *The Tacit Dimension*.

1968   Peter Drucker: *The Age of Discontinuity*. Relying on Machlup, Drucker points out that following World War II the American economy experienced a "discontinuity," a sudden shift from "goods" to "knowledge" as the trade medium.

1973   Daniel Bell: *The Coming of Post-Industrial Society*. Solidifies Machlup's and Drucker's theory that the United States has indeed moved to an "information" economy (from an industrial economy).

1986   Donald Marchand and F. Horton: *Infotrends: Profiting from Your Information Resources*. Defines knowledge management as "strategic" information management.

1986   James Beniger: *The Control Revolution: Technological and Economic Origins of the Information Society*. Traces the information age back to the industrial revolution and discusses the role of information in organisms and societies.

1988   Shoshana Zuboff: *In the Age of the Smart Machine: The Future of Work and Power*.

1988   Robert Wright: *Three Scientists and Their Gods: Looking for Meaning in an Age of Information*. In this brilliant book, Wright lays out with great clarity and wit our deepest thinking about the evolution of "information."

> "The Tree of Knowledge grew nearby."
> —Milton, *Paradise Lost*, 1667

1990   Richard Pascale: *Managing on the Edge: How the Smartest Companies Use Conflict to Stay Ahead* (includes chapter on "the two faces of learning").

1995   Ikujiro Nonaka and H. Takeuchi: *The Knowledge-Creating Company: How Japanese Companies Create the Dynamics of Innovation.*

1997   Thomas Stewart: *Intellectual Capital: The New Wealth of Organizations.*

1997   Rudy Ruggles (ed.): *Knowledge Management Tools.*

1998   Thomas Davenport and L. Prusak: *Working Knowledge: How Organizations Manage What They Know.*

1998   Carla O'Dell and C. Grayson: *If Only We Knew What We Know: Transfer of Internal Knowledge and Best Practices.*

1999   Jack Gordon: "Intellectual Capital and You," *Training* (September 1999).

2000   Nancy Dixon: *Common Knowledge: How Companies Thrive by Sharing What They Know.*

2001   Melissie Rumizen: *The Complete Idiot's Guide to Knowledge Management.*

> Tapping the brain power of the hive-mind.
> —After Mandeville:
> *The Fable of the Bees*, 1730

2001   Thomas Housel and Arthur Bell: *Measuring and Managing Knowledge.*

2001   Marc Rosenberg: *E-Learning: Strategies for Delivering Knowledge in the Digital Age.*

2002   Timothy Aeppel: "On Factory Floors, Top Workers Hide Secrets to Success: Tight-Lipped Old Hands and 'Voodoo Accuracy'," *Wall Street Journal* (July 1, 2002). Fascinating article on the challenges of capturing tacit knowledge (the "tribal lore" of employees) in the real world.

See also
Learning Objects
Learning Organization

Learning Objects

Curriculum units can be made smaller and combined with each other, like standardized mechanical building blocks, into a great variety of programs—custom-made for each learner.

> —Ralph Gerard, 1969

Break it into a thousand parts,
Yet the part is still heart-whole.

> —After Shakespeare, *As You Like It*, 1599

Definition: The Vision of Reusable Content

A new model for digital learning—one in which learning content is free from proprietary "containers," can flow among different systems and be mixed, reused, and updated continuously—is inching closer to reality. At the center of this new model is the learning object, *the modular building block.*

—Tom Barron, 2000

A learning object is a chunk of course content that can be reused in another course. It can be a paragraph, a page, or an entire lesson. An "object," in systems talk, is a "component" and learning objects "modularize" courses so that they can be re-assembled into new courses faster and cheaper. Thus learning objects function like instructional components or modular building blocks for the world of courseware. When properly designed, they constitute the fundamental "atomic particles" of the curriculum, its core components. As we will find out, however, not all courses are created equal; some contain learning objects, but many do not. Here are two examples of learning objects:

> Company A recycles a process called "Steps in Selling" from a course called "Introduction to Selling" into another course called "How to Close the Sale." The process won't change, so it can be reused in the other course with no alterations.
>
> Company B reuses an ROI formula from a sales course called "ROI-Based Selling" in another course called "ROI-Based Performance Consulting." No change to the formula is necessary; it can be recycled as is.

In both cases the chunk of content is lifted from one course and recycled in another, in a plug-and-play, drag-and-drop kind of "learning universe."

Origin and Rationale

A set is a collection of definite, distinct objects, which are elements of the whole.

—Georg Cantor, German mathematician, inventor of set theory
and godfather of object-oriented programming, 1874

Code objects let you create applications quickly, easily, and visually, including drag-and-drop control and codeless creation.
—Microsoft advertisement for its object-oriented Visual Basic, 2000

The origins of learning objects lie in the object-oriented programming movement of the 1970s and 1980s (also called structured programming). The dream of object-oriented programmers was to write code in clearly demarcated and indexed paragraphs called "objects," which could then be recycled into new programs. The vision was a compelling one, and by the early 2000s, learning strategists, information architects, and course designers caught the spirit and starting promoting the concept as a faster and cheaper way of designing and redesigning courseware. The goal was to create reusable, recyclable content, analogous to programmers creating recyclable paragraphs of code.

Perhaps the best way to describe how learning objects function is to think of them as layers in a hierarchical system, the overall system being the curriculum. The different levels or orders of the system correspond to the size or granularity of the "learning objects." If we use the analogy of a book, this becomes quite clear:

A Book Analogy	The Curriculum	Systems Theory
Entire book	Course	Superset
Chapter in book	Lesson Module	Set
Page in chapter	Page	Subset
Paragraph on a page	Paragraph	Element

Don't Confuse the Two Types of Learning Objects: Content vs. Code

When "objects" made their unobtrusive journey from backroom programmers to front-office knowledge designers and information architects, they subtly shifted their ground of reference: They went from being "code" objects to being "content" or learning objects. This has caused a considerable amount of confusion as well as set false expectations in the industry.

To explain the difference between code and content, let's take as an example a sales course written in Microsoft Word. If you're a programmer, there will be a host of code objects (subprograms) in the Word program that you could reuse (if you labeled them properly). But if you're a learning designer, there will be at most only a few concepts, checklists, and processes that you will be able to salvage in terms of content. Code is recyclable because it is explicitly designed as a set of discrete, highly structured elements: it is modular and its subsets are capable of being dragged and dropped into another course. For example, here is a chunk of Visual Basic code that is a recyclable programming "object" (it tells the program to shut down when the user clicks "exit"):

```
1: Private Sub cmdExit—
   Click ( )
2: Unload Me
3: End Sub
```

You can copy and paste this piece of code ("sub" stands for subroutine or sub-program) into your next program, and it will still perform exactly the same, for the three lines are a self-contained sub-program. Text, on the other hand, functions quite differently. Take as an example the plain sentence:

> **Technology Standards and Interoperable Learning Objects**
>
> Learning objects need to be shared among different databases and various learning management systems, and thus standards for their platform "interoperability" are absolutely essential to their proper functioning. Steps are already being taken in this direction. Programming languages such as XML—extensible markup language—and government standards such as SCORM—the sharable "content objects" reference model—are already working towards this goal. The vision is that all course content will be free of proprietary "containers" and will be able to flow freely from one course to the next. In systems terms this means an open architecture with cross-platform interoperability.

When you're with a customer, always be sure to qualify them first.

Will you recycle this sentence verbatim for the new course? Probably not. You may recycle a job aid associated with this point, such as a checklist of qualifying questions, but this particular sentence (representative of much text in a course) will probably be rewritten. Attempting to label, classify, store, and retrieve this and similar sentences is simply not worth the time and effort involved. Rewriting, (rather than recycling) is in many cases the more efficient and economical route to go. And a great deal of content falls into this category.

Words and code are not the same. If words were as discrete, specific, and modular as code is, we would be writing software programs in words. Words and sentences, however, are not stand-alone components; they are always contextually embedded in the discourse itself, anchored through syntax, narrative flow, and a semantic web. Thus text is seldom recyclable *as is*, and usually requires rewriting. To make this point clearer, let's take a look at the contrasts between words and code:

Word Objects	*Code Objects*
"learning" objects	"code" objects
data (content)	programs (containers)
embedded	independent self-contained subprograms
contextual	context-free
flow of sentences	discrete sections of code

In short, you can't merely grab content objects as "bleeding chunks" (as one critic put it), and hope that they will fall effortlessly into place in some new course. The whole reason for updating a course is generally to *update the content,* which means rewriting it. Although this point may seem obvious, many companies, caught up in the zealous pursuit of learning objects, seem not to understand it. There is a fundamental difference between content and code. The occasional pieces of content that can easily be recycled (a logo, a corporate mission statement, a company process, etc.) are often apparent to the point of being trivial, and there is no need to mount a heavy theory of learning objects to implement their recycling. When it comes to the more complex content, however, companies need to clearly determine whether it is appropriate to recycle, or whether recycling would take more time and money than it is worth.

How to Build Learning Objects

Now that we've issued all the warnings and laid down the necessary distinctions, here are the steps necessary to implement learning objects.

The Six-Step Process for Building Learning Objects

1. *Craft*

(Note: This step creates learning objects from scratch *as you are building the course.* If you built a course without learning objects in mind and are now trying to determine if there are any learning objects in it, go directly to Step 2.) First, you must craft the course. This step is often overlooked, but the actual *writing* of "componentized" courses is a different art from writing normal courses. Learning objects will be easier to recycle if your courses have been planned and written this way. The writing should be in discrete (separate) paragraphs ("objects") and in the appropriate style. Here are some rules of thumb for writing recyclable paragraphs:

- Write in a standardized corporate style so that the pieces will fit better together and the style won't jar. Think of the way the digital telephone operator pronounces numbers when you call information, using a flat robotic voice, so the numbers will mesh. Think "standard, neutral tone" of writing.
- Be brief, perhaps less than 250 words or one page. Having said this, it is a given that we all have our own definition of how long a learning object is.
- Pretend you're writing a "hyper-linked" story, meaning write each "learning object" page as a stand-alone. Think in terms of discrete chunks, not narrative or logical flow.
- Always remember that the whole point of learning objects is to recycle elements *in order to save time and money.*

2. Choose

Next select the parts of your course that are most likely to be reused. Definitions, processes, and company checklists are among the information types that are "less volatile." Products and services courses are less likely to have stable content.

3. Chunk

Chunk the selected course parts into layers and components of layers, similar to a hierarchical outline (don't be confused by the technical words for this phase—decomposition, deconstruction, componentization, and modularization—they all mean the same thing). In doing this, you will be determining at what level of granularity learning objects will be defined. Some companies refer to lessons and modules as learning objects, others to paragraph-level or even Webscreen-sized chunks. Obviously the size of a "learning object" lies in the eye of the beholder. Take your pick and stick with it.

4. Classify

Next classify the components, labeling each of them appropriately in accordance with the naming conventions that you set up in conjunction with your IT department (and their indexing system for the database). Learning objects must be meta-tagged—listed in a master index under keyword, subject matter, media, audience, and so on (these are equivalent to the fields or attributes listed in a database)—if they are to be readily retrievable in the future. The entire process is a form of knowledge management.

5. *Configure*
Set up the database schema (outline or model) for the ready storage and retrieval of the components.

6. *Catalog*
Finally, import the components into the system ("populate the database").

Conclusion: Getting Real

This is a utopian goal: travelers should approach it with caution.
                    —Walker and Hess, *Instructional Software,* 1984

Learning objects will work for you, as I have said, if you proceed logically. To help set you on the right path, there are two strategies you can adopt as you follow the six-step process above, namely the inverse law and the 10-percent solution.

The Inverse Law

This strategy derives from an old saw: " 'Faster, cheaper, better'—pick any two!" This is particularly true for learning objects, for if they theoretically create curriculums "faster and cheaper," they probably won't create curriculums that are also "better." The new courses, made from recycled parts, may be sufficient, but their quality will probably be that of, say, generic off-the-shelf courseware. This may be appropriate for some courses, but not for others. Implementations of learning objects necessitate a simplification of courses and usually will imply a lowest common denominator in terms of quality; expect this, and you will not be disappointed.

The 10 Percent Solution (and the Usual Warnings About Techno-Utopianism)

This strategy consists of telling yourself that you'll be happy if you can recycle 10 percent of your courses. It would be foolhardy, for instance, to expect content to remain so stagnant as to be 50 percent recyclable for next year's courses. As you proceed with the recycling process, keep a rough log of what percentage and what types of content you actually do rescue from past courses, continue to correct your expectations, and celebrate the small triumphs. And be sure to push back on any techno-utopians in your organization by reminding them that it's easier to create object-oriented *code* than object-oriented *content* (and ask them how they're coming with their own object-oriented programming efforts). Get real, have fun with learning objects, and don't let anybody push you around.

What's in a Name?

Learning objects go by a variety of names, including the following:
    Content chunks
    Content objects
    Info-nuggets
    Infotrons
    Instructional components
    Instructional objects
    Knowledge components
    Knowledge objects
    Knowledge quanta
    Learning nuggets
    Learning particles
    Repurposed content
    Reusable information objects (RIOs)
    Reusable learning objects (RLOs)
All of these refer to the same thing.

FASTPATHS

1874   German mathematician Georg Cantor invents set theory, including the notion of "objects"—which will become the theoretical basis of object-oriented programming a full century later.

1966   Ole-Johan Dahl and Kristen Nygaard: "Simula: An Algol-Based Simulation Language," *Communications of the ACM* 9 (1966): 671–678. One of the first articles on the need for object-oriented programming languages. Authors' "algol" language was a forerunner of such object-oriented languages as C++, which was developed at Bell Labs in the 1980s. This "object orientation" would pass directly into the thinking about learning objects in the 1990s.

1969   Richard Atkinson and H. A. Wilson (eds.): *Computer-Assisted Instruction.* One of a number of (still very relevant) structured programming books on CAI from the 1960s and 1970s. Contains the 1969 article by Gerard,

"Shaping the Mind: Computers in Education," from which the motto at the beginning of this section is taken.

1970s   Growth of object-oriented programming (paralleling a related wave of object-oriented "new math" teaching at the time).

1976   Franklin DeRemer and H. Kron: "Programming-in-the-Large vs. Programming-in-the-Small," *IEEE Transactions on Software Engineering,* June 1976, pp. 80–86. One example of the many articles in the 1970s promoting structured, recyclable programming, whose ideas are still absolutely relevant and applicable today. Programmers should work with standard components, programming in the large, with a decreased need for programming in the small; they should program on the level of the "forest," not individual "trees."

1982   Anthony Wasserman and Steven Gutz: "The Future of Programming," *Communications of the ACM;* reprinted in Walker and Hess (1984). Compelling argument for reusable learning objects in programming.

1983–1985   Object-oriented programming gains headway; the language C++ is created at AT&T's Bell Labs.

1984   Decker Walker and Robert Hess (eds.): *Instructional Software: Principles for Design and Use.* Like the Atkinson anthology, still relevant today.

1990   David Schneider: *Microsoft QuickPascal: An Introduction to Structured and Object-Oriented Programming.* For programming types only; helps explain the theory lying behind learning objects.

1990s   Object-oriented databases are developed (as opposed to relational databases). The decade also saw the development of more object-oriented programming languages beyond C++, namely Mac's Hypercard, Microsoft's Visual Basic, and Sun's Java.

1990   Won Kim: *Introduction to Object-Oriented Databases.* For programming types only; helps explain the theory lying behind learning objects.

2000s   "Learning objects" are promoted as a faster, cheaper way of designing and developing online courses.

2002   David Wiley (ed.): *The Instructional Use of Learning Objects.* Useful, if academically-oriented, articles on learning objects by various hands.

See also
Electronic Performance Support
Job Aids
Knowledge Management

Learning Organization

The Learning Organization could not become a reality until the coming of the World Wide Web and the engines of strategic assessment.
—David H. Miles, 2003

A learning organization is any organization that fosters continuous learning on both the organizational and individual levels, in order to improve performance. The continuous learning is based on twin feedback loops, permitting the organization to learn while individual employees learn as well. (See Double Loop Learning.) Overall, the organization is viewed as a living organism, complete with feedback systems and the ability to adapt to change in its environment.

FASTPATHS

1969   Peter Drucker: *The Age of Discontinuity.* Drucker points out that we are shifting from a corporate culture based on physical labor to one depending on a knowledge society, a transition from an industrial society to an information one. The first inklings that organizations must continuously learn to adapt to change.

1970   Alvin Toffler's *Future Shock* outlines the shift from industrialism to informationalism, stressing the ability to change and learn.

1971   Donald Schon: *Beyond the Stable State.* A brilliant, little known book on learning organizations, systems, and processes, twenty years before their popularity in instructional circles. Schon argues that rapidly accelerating change is undermining the stability of our society; institutions must become learning "systems," maintaining flexibility and adapting to situations as they arise. Corporations should organize themselves around functions and processes rather than products and tasks.

1978   Chris Argyris and Donald Schon: *Organizational Learning I.* Abstract, academic, and difficult to read, but important because it starts to move the discussion beyond training to learning in organizations.

1982   Reginald Revans: *The Origins and Growth of Action Learning.* The great master of action learning, as it relates to organizational learning.

1983   Rosabeth Kanter: *The Change Masters: Innovation for Productivity in the American Corporation.* Studies of entrepreneurship and the ability to adapt quickly inside large corporations.

1987   Marvin Weisbord: *Productive Workplaces.* Prologue is excellent on "learning how to learn" in the 1960s, and on the importance of "lessons learned"—always asking "what did we learn from that?"

1990   The Learning Organization is officially born simultaneously in three separate books:

■ Charles Handy: *The Age of Unreason.* The British standpoint. See chapter on "Re-Inventing Education."

■ Richard Pascale: *Managing on the Edge.* The view from Stanford. A superb study.

■ Peter Senge: *The Fifth Discipline: The Art and Practice of the Learning Organization.* A theorist from MIT, utilizing MIT systems theory.

2000   David Garvin: *Learning in Action: A Guide to Putting the Learning Organization to Work.*

See also
Action Learning
Lessons Learned
Organizational Development

Learning Strategy

Learning strategy refers to the instructional strategy used in a course, the framework or methodology employed to lay out the material and impart learning to the student. Most learning strategies, no matter how complex, are ultimately based on a fundamental three-step process:

1. Teach
2. Practice
3. Test

When amplified, this process translates into:

1. Presentation of material; colloquially, "show and tell"
2. Experiential exercises or applied scenarios
3. Feedback through assessments

Methodological Foundations

This fundamental strategy or process, based on Herbart's nineteenth-century five-step learning theory, was first deployed on a widespread basis by trainers in 1914, during the early days of World War I. Although the model has since been modified, the basic principles remain the same. It should be noted that, because of the ambiguity of the word "learning," a learning strategy sometimes refers to the *student's* method of learning (previewing the material, reading it, and reviewing it) rather than the teacher's teaching strategy.

> *See also*
> Herbart
> Instructional Systems Design

Learning Style

The Modalities of Learning

Your learning style is your preferred method of learning—your favored medium and method. There is no agreement among experts as to how to classify and categorize styles. We list several of them here.

■ *Senses*: Many people favor a particular medium when learning. Some learn best by watching, others through listening, and still others through physically doing. These sensory modalities are called visual, auditory, and tactile or kinesthetic.

■ *Structure*: Within each preferred sense or modality there are further distinctions, in particular with regard to *structure*. Some students prefer story-driven scenarios, others the challenge of a problem, still others rational pathways. These are known as narrative, problem-solving, and logical learning styles.

■ *Social Context*: Some students learn better alone; others in small groups; still others in large groups.

■ *Blends*: Finally, there are the obvious blends of the foregoing learning styles, and often these depend as much upon the subject matter as the personal learning style.

Kolb's Four Learning Styles

An influential study of learning styles was written in 1984 by David Kolb, in which he lays out his own classification of perceptual modalities, information processing styles, and personality patterns. Influenced strongly by the experiential learning theories of John Dewey, Kurt Lewin, and Jean Piaget, Kolb develops the following four styles:

- ■ *Activist Style*: prefers hands-on case studies and simulations
- ■ *Reflector Style*: prefers lectures and then brainstorming
- ■ *Theorist Style*: prefers conceptual readings
- ■ *Pragmatist Style*: prefers field work in the workplace

Practical Applications

The challenge with learning styles lies not in their theory, or even in the fact that experts can't agree on classifications, but in their application. Time and money legislate against constructing courses on a multiple "learning style" basis (each version having different sensory pathways). It would be extremely expensive to produce separate video, audiocassette, and story-driven versions of each course.

FASTPATHS

1984   David Kolb: *Experiential Learning: Experience as the Source of Learning and Development.*

See also
Multiple intelligences

Lessons Learned

If caught in a minefield, don't turn around! Instead, back out.
—*A Lesson Learned*, U.S. Army, 1997

Background: Postmortems

"Lessons learned" are project debriefs, which are sometimes referred to as "postmortems." These debriefs, held at the end of a project with the full team, collect a list of what went wrong, what went right, and what one can do to improve procedures the next time around. Typical items showing up on project debriefs include avoiding scope creep (adding features but not allotting time or budget to build them) and better management of expectations for the project.

The only problem with postmortems is that the vast majority of recommendations that come out of them are never implemented, ending up in the corporate morgue, the backroom filing cabinets, or someone's hard drive—one more round of perfunctory rituals in a bureaucratic organization with *no teeth because there is no follow-on reinforcement.*

Turning Point: "Fighting a One-Year Battle Nine Times in a Row"

In the 1980s, however, an unlikely group paved the way for putting lessons learned into action, namely the U.S. Army, one of the most bureaucratic organizations on earth. The Army had made an important discovery: In Vietnam, rather than fighting a nine-year war, they had in effect fought a one-year battle nine times over. Because of officer-rotation policies, there had been no carryover of lessons learned from one mission to the next.

As a result of these findings and in order to mount a continuous learning architecture, the Army in 1985 founded the Center for Army Lessons Learned. Similar to postmortems and project wrap up meetings, this group began to compile lessons learned from "after-action reviews" in the field. The next step the army took was to devise a system for actually applying these "lessons learned" back in the field. They began by distributing them back to the field through e-mails, for application on the next mission. As a Harvard Business School case study reported, "the Army perfected a remarkably efficient process for correcting mistakes and sustaining successes" (see Fastpaths 1997, Ricks).

Continuous Learning: The Four-Step Process

Sweeping metaphors and grand themes are far less helpful than the knowledge of how individuals and organizations learn on a daily basis. The key to success is mastery of details.

—David Garvin

The lessons-learned process, first modeled by the U.S. Army, is a simple one and consists of four steps:

1. *Collect.* Collect the lessons learned using live interviews, group debriefs, and e-mailed questionnaires.
2. *Compile.* Select and edit the lessons.
3. *Distribute.* Disseminate to project leaders or targeted personnel.
4. *Enforce Application to New Projects.* This is the key point in the entire process. Rewards, recognitions, and compensation are in order to help support follow-through.

A Challenge to Organizational Inertia

Although lessons learned is a simple concept, problems can arise with reinforcement of the lessons. Organizations are better at maintaining the status quo than learning and changing. They may pay lip service to learning from experience or continuous process improvement, and yet do nothing about it. But implementation of even the most basic "lessons learned" can bring about enormous rewards in terms of organizational efficiency. Moreover, the infrastructure involved can be as simple as a Word document on an e-mail system. The lessons-learned field (and its potential ROI) is still largely untapped.

FASTPATHS

1997 Thomas Ricks: "Lessons Learned: Army Devises System to Decide What Does, and Does Not, Work: Corporate America Watches with Interest," *Wall Street Journal* (May 23, 1997).

2000   David Garvin: *Learning in Action: A Guide to Putting the Learning Organization to Work.*

See also
Action Learning

A hard lesson—that may do thee good.
                            —Shakespeare, *Much Ado About Nothing,* 1600

Likert Scale

In 1932, Rensis Likert published *A Technique for the Measurement of Attitudes,* introducing the Likert Scale. This now ubiquitous five-point scale measures attitudes by asking participants to answer using numbers 1 through 5, from "strongly disagree" through "disagree," "neutral," and "agree," to "strongly agree." The instrument has remained a staple of the rating industry as well as of training feedback sheets, down to the present day.

FASTPATHS

1932   Rensis Likert: *A Technique for the Measurement of Attitudes.*

Management Theory, People-Centered

Douglas McGregor and Humanistic Management (Theory Y)

The humanistic or human relations theory of management, which started to emerge in the 1920s and 1930s and came into full flower during the 1960s, focuses on small group improvements within an organization in a "bottom up" approach to organizational improvement. The term "humanistic" in this context refers to a heightened emphasis on the employee's quality of work life and job satisfaction, through such strategies as participative management. In place of a "command and control" structure, human relations management theory fosters self-directed teams and grass roots efforts. The major themes of the movement—change management, team building, enhanced communications, conflict resolution interventions, and increased individual responsibilities—have a familiar ring to them because they have passed into the language by now, and lie at the heart of modern organization development, the discipline that inherited the best and the brightest of these ideas in the 1960s and 1970s. (See Organizational Development.)

The field of players in the humanistic movement include Kurt Lewin, father of organizational development, Elton Mayo, the 1950s psychologists Carl Rogers and Abraham Maslow, and Douglas McGregor from the early 1960s. It was McGregor who came up with the slogan for the humanist group, namely "Theory Y." Theory Y, with its kinder gentler humanism, was the successor to the preceding generation's "Theory X," which, spearheaded by Frederick Taylor, had preached a scientific management to an industrial age. (See Hawthorne Effect; Management Theory, Process-Centered; and Maslow's Hierarchy of Needs.)

The best of all possible management worlds would combine the best of Taylor with the best of the human relations group and its successor, organizational development. The fusion of these two management theories would carry much power in terms of performance improvement. Marvin Weisbord, in fact, in his *Productive Workplaces*, charts just how complementary—if not directly overlapping—the two movements are (see Fastpaths 1987, Weisbord).

FASTPATHS

1920   Kurt Lewin publishes article on the "Humanization of the Taylor System." Lewin, educated in Viennese Gestalt psychology (which studied the relationships between individuals and groups), flees Hitler in the 1930s and emigrates to the United States. Reacting against the mechanistic, authoritarian view of organizations ("management from above")—as supposedly exemplified in Frederick Taylor's *Principles of Scientific Management* of 1911—Lewin focuses on the organic growth of organizations from within (through "bottom up" small group efforts). Where Taylor stressed "plan, measure, and control," Lewin stresses "participate and collaborate." Where Freud viewed behavior as being dictated by a person's past and Skinner would see behavior being influenced by an employee's future rewards, Lewin (from his grounding in Gestalt psychology) stressed present interactions between the individual and the group in the everyday workplace. In 1939 he coined the term *group dynamics,* and he would go on in the 1940s and 1950s to found the discipline of organizational development.

1933   Elton Mayo: *The Human Problems of an Industrial Civilization.* Mayo's reports on the "Hawthorne effect." (See Hawthorne Effect.)

1935   Kurt Lewin: *A Dynamic Theory of Personality.*

1936   Kurt Lewin: *Principles of Topological Psychology.*

1938   Chester Barnard: *The Functions of the Executive.* A classic synthesis work, combining Taylor's "scientific management" with the "humanistic" school of thought.

1943   Abraham Maslow, a humanist psychologist, publishes "The Theory of Human Motivation" in the *Psychological Review.* This is Maslow's first paper on his well-known "hierarchy of needs." (See Maslow's Hierarchy of Needs.)

1945   Kurt Lewin forms a research center at MIT to study "group dynamics"—group behavior in organizations. Lewin's studies of leadership styles encourage participative management techniques in organizational development, and eventually lead to MIT professor Douglas McGregor's work on the human side of management (see Fastpaths 1960, McGregor).

1946   Peter Drucker publishes *The Concept of the Corporation.* Based on his analyses of General Motors, Drucker's work launches his American career. Drucker, picking up where his hero Frederick Taylor had left off in 1911, helps invent the role of the management consultant and the field of American management theory.

1950   David Riesman, sociologist of human relations, publishes *The Lonely Crowd: A Study of the Changing American Character.* Riesman sets up a typology of three historical figures in American business: the tradition-directed agrarian worker, the "inner-directed" pioneer employee of the industrial era, and the "other-directed" manager of the 1950s, who relies on peer-group pressures.

1951   Carl Rogers, psychiatrist, publishes *Client-Centered Therapy,* and launches the humanist movement in psychology, where the client-centered perspective helps boost the employee-focused trend within organizational development and which would culminate in McGregor's humanist management theories in 1960.

1951   Edward C. Tolman: *Behavior and Psychological Man: Essays in Motivation and Learning.*

1954   Abraham Maslow: *Motivation and Personality.* Landmark book in Maslow's developing ideas about the importance and complexity of human motivation (see also Fastpaths 1943, Maslow; 1955, Whyte; 1960, McGregor; and 1964, Vroom).

1954 Peter Drucker: *The Practice of Management.*

1950s Eric Trist and Fred Emery of the Tavistock Institute of Human Relations in England, influenced by Lewin, also engage in the study of group dynamics and socio-technical systems (the interaction of people with technology). Their theory views organizations as "open systems," living organisms interacting with their environments. (See Systems: An Architecture of Continuous Learning Systems.)

1955 William F. Whyte (ed.): *Money and Motivation.* To achieve optimum output from employees, one must consider motivation as well as money (see Fastpaths 1964, Vroom).

1956 William F. Whyte's classic *The Organization Man* argues that American business life has abandoned old-style individualism in favor of "the organization man" and a bureaucratic ethic of security, loyalty, and conformity. With the rise of the new postwar corporation, American individualism is fast disappearing from mainstream middle-class life. The organization man will become McGregor's traditional "Theory X" man (see Fastpaths 1960, McGregor).

1957 Robert Tannenbaum and Warren Schmidt: "How to Choose a Leadership Pattern," *Harvard Business Review* (March–April 1957). Theory of a leadership continuum from authoritarian to democratic styles—and thus a precursor of McGregor's management continuum from Theory X to Theory Y (see Fastpaths 1960, McGregor).

1958 McGregor and Beckhard, building on the work of Kurt Lewin, coin the term "organization development." (See Organizational Development.)

1959 Frederick Herzberg, B. Mausner, B. Snyderman: *The Motivation to Work.* One of the founding texts on motivation, republished several times, and still relevant.

1960 Douglas McGregor (1906–1964): *The Human Side of Enterprise.* Following Maslow (1943), Rogers (1951), Whyte (1956), and Tannenbaum (1957), McGregor formulates two theories of human nature—and thereby a new generalized theory of human management.

The first, older theory, Theory X, represents the old-fashioned authoritarian "tough manager" belief that "human beings dislike work and will avoid it if they can," and generally supports a punitive management of criticism and control. This is often falsely associated with Taylor's "scientific" management of 1911 and with what Maslow described as the "security mindedness" of American labor unions in the 1950s.

The second theory, Theory Y, offers McGregor's alternative, the democratic "soft manager" view that human "expenditure of effort at work is as natural as play" and hence supports a motivational management of rewards and recognitions. This theory builds on Lewin's humanistic management theories as well as on Maslow's description of our need for "self-esteem" and "self-actualization" (1943, 1954). In Theory Y, participative problem solving replaces military-style directives.

McGregor's book, its message well timed to its appearance at the beginning of the liberal 1960s, meets with huge success and becomes a management classic. The more fascinating truth about McGregor's Theory X and Theory Y, however, is that the workplace actually requires a creative combination of both points of view in order to function properly (see Fastpaths 1987, Weisbord).

1964 Victor Vroom: *Work and Motivation.* Helps popularize Kurt Lewin's work in social psychology, organizational development, and motivation (see also Fastpaths 1920 and 1945, Lewin; 1954, Maslow; and 1955, Whyte).

1969 Ken Blanchard and Paul Hersey: *Management of Organizational Behavior.* Excellent summary of management theory including motivation, environment, leadership, situational variables, and overall organizational effectiveness.

1969 Alfred Marrow: *The Practical Theorist: The Life and Work of Kurt Lewin*

1982 Tom Peters and Bob Waterman: *In Search of Excellence.* Kicks off the management guru wave of the 1980s, 1990s, and 2000s. The book, by two former McKinsey consultants, preached "stay close to the customer and create customer-value, stick to your knitting," etc.

1983 Rosabeth Kanter: *The Change Masters.* Studies of entrepreneurship inside large corporations.

1985 Ken Blanchard: *Leadership and the One-Minute Manager: Increasing Effectiveness Through Situational Leadership.*

1987 Marvin Weisbord: *Productive Workplaces.* An extraordinarily readable account of the rise of human relations management and organizational development.

1995 William Rothwell: *Practicing Organization Development.*

See also
Hawthorne Effect
Management Theory, Process-Centered
Organizational Development

Management Theory, Process-Centered

Frederick Taylor and Scientific Management (Theory X)

Frederick Taylor's accomplishment is the most powerful as well as the most lasting contribution America has made to Western thought since the Federalist Papers.
—Peter Drucker, *The Practice of Management*, 1954

"Scientific," or process-centered, management theory begins with Frederick Taylor (1856–1915), a brilliant engineer at the turn of the last century who invented not only the modern professions of performance improvement and management consulting, but also time management and process-centered systems engineering. Starting in the 1880s and working with such industrial giants of the time as Bethlehem Steel, Taylor pioneered time-and-motion studies in order to streamline processes on the assembly lines and improve performance in the shops and work yards. The scientific aspect of his process reengineering consisted of dividing tasks into their smallest subcomponents, and then enforcing strict performance specifications for each task, as well as gearing the system's tools to support the task as well.

Unfortunately many of Taylor's principles would be pushed aside in the 1930s by the "human relations" movement of Kurt Lewin and Elton Mayo, and in the 1950s by Abraham Maslow and Carl Rogers—all of them forerunners of organizational development. Not until the 1980s does Taylor's heritage surface again in Deming's Total Quality Management (TQM) movement and in the 1990s with Hammer's process reengineering. Today, Taylor's scientific ideas (dubbed Theory X by McGregor) are best viewed as being complementary to the humanist theories of organizational development (McGregor's own Theory Y), for the rigor of Taylor's systems engineering approach needs to be balanced out by the people-centered strategies of OD. Each theory stands in need of the other, and both benefit from their fusion. When viewed in this larger light, Taylor, as Peter Drucker has emphasized, stands out as one of the great masters of twentieth-century management theory and practice.

FASTPATHS

1903 Frederick Taylor's *Shop Management* appears, an early version of his later 1911 work, *The Principles of Scientific Management*. Addresses the systems side of manufacturing organizations, prescribing breaking out system operations into component subprocesses and tasks for subsequent analysis and performance improvement.

1908 Harvard Business School is founded, and proclaims Taylor's scientific management theory as "the new revolution."

1911 Frederick Taylor's *Principles of Scientific Management* appears. The book lays out a process-centered systems engineering model for the industrial age, including time and motion studies. As a pioneer of scientific management, Taylor is often denounced as rigid and authoritarian (particularly by those who have not actually read him), but this is a misconception, as the very opening statement of his book indicates: "The principal object of management should be to secure the maximum prosperity for the employer coupled with maximum prosperity for each employee." Taylor goes on to describe the four major elements of his scientific management:

1. Engineering of processes

2. Appropriate training and development

3. Cooperation of management with employees to ensure quality

4. An equal division of work and responsibility between management and employees

Moreover, Taylor's gap analyses—looking for the differential between "what is" and "what ought to be"—foreshadows by a century what performance improvement systems are accomplishing today. At a slender 140 pages, Taylor's book packs more punch than many modern management books three times its size. Nor do you have to agree with the book in order to benefit enormously.

1916 Henri Fayol: *General and Industrial Management*. French management theorist. Together with the American Frederick Taylor, known as "fathers of modern management." Formulates five functions of management: Plan, Organize, Command, Coordinate, and Control.

1923 Frank Copley: *Frederick W. Taylor: Father of Scientific Management*. A family-sanctioned biography, so needs to be read carefully, but extremely useful details.

1954 Peter Drucker: *The Practice of Management*, 1954. Praises Taylor as one of the great thinkers of the modern corporate world.

1976 Peter Drucker: "The Coming Rediscovery of Scientific Management" in *The Conference Board Record* (June 1976, pp. 23–27). Drucker views Taylor as one of the great makers of the modern corporate world.

1980 D. Nelson: *Frederick W. Taylor and the Rise of Scientific Management.*

1987 Marvin Weisbord: *Productive Workplaces.* Very readable history of management theory, including two chapters on Taylor and scientific management, with an interesting exposition of the surprisingly close affinities between Taylor's scientific management and McGregor's later human relations management in the 1960s.

1991 Stephen Waring: *Taylorism Transformed: Scientific Management Theory Since 1945.*

1991 Charles Wrege and R. Greenwood: *Frederick W. Taylor: The Father of Scientific Management.*

1997 Robert Kanigel: *The One Best Way: Frederick Winslow Taylor and the Enigma of Efficiency.* Superlative modern biography of Taylor, viewing him, as Peter Drucker had, as the source of our continuing focus in the twenty-first century on performance improvement, efficiency, and effectiveness in organizations.

See also
Management Theory, People-Centered
Reengineering
Total Quality Management

Maslow's Hierarchy of Needs

Abraham Maslow (1908–1970), one of the founders of humanistic psychology, developed a theory of self-actualization, but is best known in business circles for his hierarchy of human needs, a systems-oriented classification of human factors influencing employee motivation. The best way to recall Maslow's hierarchy is to arrange it within William James' three levels of human needs (material, social, and spiritual). The hierarchy looks like this:

I. Material Needs
   1. Physical needs: food, clothing, and shelter
   2. Safety needs: freedom from physical danger

II. Social Needs
   3. The need to belong to a group, to be accepted
   4. The need for esteem, to achieve and be recognized by the group
III. Spiritual Needs
   5. The need to know, to understand (cognitive exploration)
   6. The need for aesthetic experience (symmetry, order, beauty)
   7. The need for self-actualization (realizing one's potential)
   8. The need for spiritual experience (religious transcendence)

Higher needs, Maslow states, can't be addressed until lower needs are satisfied; and a need, once satisfied, is no longer a motivator. Maslow's 1943 article and his subsequent book (1954) exert a powerful influence on training and development, particularly with respect to motivation studies in the 1950s and the rise of organizational development (and theories of organizational needs) in the 1960s.

FASTPATHS

1943 "The Theory of Human Motivation," Maslow's first paper on the hierarchy of needs, appears in *The Psychological Review*.

1950 *Self-Actualizing People: A Study of Psychological Health*

1954 *Motivation and Personality.* Landmark book that presents Maslow's developing ideas about motivation and needs.

1962 *Toward a Psychology of Being*

1964 *Religions, Values, and Peak-Experiences*

1965 *Eupsychian Management*

1971 *The Farther Reaches of Human Nature*

1998 *Maslow on Management* (edited by Deborah Stephens and Gary Heil)

Multiple Intelligences

Such intelligence hath seldom failed.
—Shakespeare, *All's Well That Ends Well*, 1602

The Seven Intelligences

The Greeks cultivated the seven lively arts, the Middle Ages the seven deadly sins, and the twenty-first century enjoys the seven lively intelligences. In a book that appeared in 1983 called *Frames of Mind*, Howard Gardner, an ex-Harvard pupil of cognitive psychologist Joseph Bruner, went up against the psychological establishment and proposed that there were more intelligences "on heaven and earth" than the standard verbal-and-math scores were telling us. Gardner's definition of an intelligence is *the ability to solve a problem or create a product that is valued by a particular organization*. Each of us possesses a unique blend of "intelligences" (a cognitive or mental profile) that we develop and draw upon throughout our lives.

Seven Windows of the Mind

Gardner, going up against cognitive psychologists such as Piaget, is a pluralist. He believes we possess more than one or two intellectual competences (mental abilities) and what's more, he names them. There are seven, and through these seven windows the mind processes its information from the outside world. These seven are:

- *Bodily-Kinesthetic*: Physical intelligence as exhibited by athletes and sports leaders.
- *Interpersonal*: Social intelligence as exhibited by therapists, politicians, and great leaders.
- *Intrapersonal*: Self-awareness as in the ability of a Freud or a Jung to analyze themselves, or of writers to write about their own inner lives. This includes a fuller knowledge and awareness of one's own feelings and emotions.
- *Linguistic*: Traditional academic verbal skills.
- *Logical-Mathematical*: Traditional academic math skills.
- *Musical*: Shared by composers and performers from Mozart to Stravinsky.
- *Spatial*: Shared by architects, painters, and similar professions.

Is There an Eighth Intelligence?

In 1990 Peter Salovey and John Mayer, inspired by Gardner, suggested an eighth intelligence, namely "emotional intelligence." Daniel Goleman has since followed this up with several books on the topic. And in 1999

Gardner proposed his own eighth intelligence, namely classificatory intelligence. Such an intelligence is demonstrated by information theorists, database designers, and even botanists and zoologists (Charles Darwin, Audubon, Linnaeus, and Aristotle). At the heart of this intelligence lies the ability to identify and classify vast fields of knowledge, information, and data.

How Do Intelligences Relate to Learning Styles and Competencies?

Because of the newness of the discipline of multiple intelligences (MI), certain overlaps exist between these and more traditional performance descriptors, such as learning styles and competencies. At this time it is probably best to consider multiple intelligences close cousins of learning styles as well as of competencies. Visual and auditory "learning styles," for instance, are obviously the basis, respectively, for spatial and musical intelligences.

Outlook

The study of multiple intelligences is a new discipline, still in the exploratory phase. It shares with learning styles and competencies the fact that it is still largely descriptive, classificatory, and theoretical rather than applied. One of the great benefits of Gardner's breakthrough, however, is that he has cleansed the doors of perception to what *real* intelligences are involved in the different types of performance. He has opened our eyes and it is up to the performance improvers to follow through with designing real-world solutions based on the theory.

FASTPATHS

1883   Francis Galton: *Inquiries into Human Faculty.* Galton, a cousin of Charles Darwin, pioneers the study of the varieties of human intelligence.

1912   Alfred Binet and T. Simon: *The Development of Intelligence in Children.* Two French psychologists set the agenda for the classic view of intelligence that will hold through most of the twentieth century—namely that aptitude can be measured by scores on an IQ test with verbal and math components.

1960   L. Thurstone: *The Nature of Intelligence.* A mental pluralist, Thurstone posits seven "vectors of the mind."

1967   J. Guilford: *The Nature of Human Intelligence.* Posits multiple "factors" of the intellect.

1983   J. Fodor: *The Modularity of Mind.* Investigates different domains or modules of the mind beyond the standard verbal and mathematical domains.

1983   Howard Gardner: *Frames of Mind: The Theory of Multiple Intelligences.* Sets forth the theory of the seven intelligences. Difficult to read at times, but provides a refreshingly new angle on the world of performance and work.

1993   Howard Gardner: *Creating Minds: An Anatomy of Creativity Seen Through the Lives of Freud, Einstein, Picasso, Stravinsky, Eliot, Graham, and Gandhi.* Gardner illustrates several of the seven intelligences through biographies of famous practitioners.

1993   Howard Gardner: *Multiple Intelligences: The Theory in Practice.* Follow-up reader on the multiple intelligences, put together by Gardner and his students at Harvard.

1995   Howard Gardner et al.: *Leading Minds: An Anatomy of Leadership.* Anthology of views on "leadership" intelligence.

1995   Daniel Goleman: *Emotional Intelligence: Why It Can Matter More Than IQ.* Suggests an eighth intelligence. (See Emotional Intelligence.)

1996   Howard Gardner and others: *Intelligence: Multiple Perspectives.*

1999   Howard Gardner: *Intelligence Reframed: Multiple Intelligences for the Twenty-first Century.* Gardner adds his own eighth intelligence: "naturalist" or classificatory intelligence.

See also
Competencies
Emotional Intelligence
Learning Style

Organizational Development

Originating in the late 1950s and early 1960s, organizational development—or frequently "organization development"—focuses on the "human side" of corporations rather than on the scientific management side (see Management Theory, People-Centered and Management Theory, Process-Centered). Building on the socio-technical systems theory of

Emery and Trist in England (which studied people, technology, and processes), the social psychology of Kurt Lewin, Carl Rogers, and Abraham Maslow in America, and the humanist experiments of Elton Mayo (see Hawthorne Effect), OD champions a view of workers as active participants in organizations rather than as links in a passive assembly line. Expanding Training and Development's traditional mandate of developing individual staff members, OD takes as its province the development of entire organizations. One way to view OD initially, in fact, is to see it as being a complement to the traditional view of training; here is a listing of the two, side by side:

Training	Organizational Development
Tactical teachers	Strategic consultants
Deliver courses	Facilitate groups
Trainer	Change agent (change management)
Build individual skills	Build teams, resolve conflicts
Hold classes	Carry out interventions
Lower level audience	Executive audience
Ad hoc events	Long-term relationships
Reactive	Proactive
Target knowledge	Target change

Having said this for purposes of differentiation, we should probably add that the two worlds are now fast coming together because of their common goal of "performance improvement." Entire HR departments are now calling themselves departments of organizational development, with their mandate being employee development as well as "organizational" development.

FASTPATHS

Best Introduction:

W. Warner Burke: *Organizational Development: A Process of Learning and Changing* (1993, available in a more recent edition).

Best Series:

Addison-Wesley series on Organization Development (started by Beckhard and Schein in the 1960s).

Best History of Movement:

> Marvin Weisbord: *Productive Workplaces* (1987), including chapter on "McGregor and the Roots of Organization Development." An inspired introduction to the rise of modern management theories and organizational development from Taylor's scientific management through Kurt Lewin's OD to McGregor's humanistic management and to more recent trends. Highly recommended for all performance consultants, instructional designers, and human performance technologists. One of the clearest books in the field, and written with passion, empathy, and understanding. Not only is Weisbord's book the best critical history of the OD movement, but it also highlights some surprising similarities between OD and earlier Taylorism.

Rapid History of the Movement as a Whole:

1911   Frederick Taylor: *Principles of Scientific Management.* Taylor's theory is typical of the old-line mechanistic view of organizations that OD initially reacted against (instead following in the footsteps of such thinkers and theorists as Kurt Lewin).

1951   Kurt Lewin: *Field Theory in Social Science.* Organization development is Lewin's living monument, and this book shows why. Lewin anticipates all the major themes of OD: team building, leadership styles, participative management, consultation skills, and change management (see Fastpaths 1987, Weisbord).

> McGregor and Beckhard, building on the work of Lewin and others, reportedly coined the term "organizational development" in 1958.

1959   Fred Emery: *The Emergence of a New Paradigm of Work.*

1960   Douglas McGregor: *The Human Side of Enterprise.*

1963   Eric Trist: *Organizational Choice.*

1964   Peter Drucker: *Managing for Results.* Vintage Drucker.

1964   Victor Vroom: *Work and Motivation.*

1965   Edgar Schein: *Organizational Psychology.*

1969   Richard Beckhard: *Organization Development: Strategies and Models.*

1969   Edgar Schein: *Process Consultation: Its Role in Organization Development.*

1969   Paul Hersey and Ken Blanchard: *Management of Organizational Behavior: Utilizing Human Resources.*

1970   Robert Townsend: *Up the Organization.* A delightfully lighthearted and iconoclastic look at organizations. Recommended reading still.

1972   Fred E. Emery and Russell Ackoff: *On Purposeful Systems.*

1972   Wendell French and Cecil Bell: *Organization Development: Behavioral Science Interventions for Organization Improvement.*

1977   Jay Galbraith: *Organization Design.*

1978   Donald Schon and C. Argyris: *Organizational Learning I and II.*

1978   Wendell French (ed.): *Organization Development: Theory, Practice, and Research.*

1978   Marvin Weisbord: *Organizational Diagnosis: A Workbook of Theory and Practice.*

1981   Peter Block: *Flawless Consulting.*

1982   W. Warner Burke *Organization Development: Principles and Practices.*

1983   Rosabeth Kanter: *The Change Masters.* Kanter studies the potential for entrepreneurship inside large corporations.

1987   James Kouzes and B. Posner: *The Leadership Challenge.*

1987   Marvin Weisbord: *Productive Workplaces.*

1987   Michael Harrison: *Diagnosing Organizations.*

1988   David Hanna: *Designing Organizations for High Performance.*

1990   Richard Pascale: *Managing on the Edge: How the Smartest Companies Use Conflict to Stay Ahead.*

1991   Lee Bolman and T. Deal: *Reframing Organizations.*

1993   Richard Pascale et al.: "The Reinvention Roller Coaster," *Harvard Business Review* (November–December 1993). Urges organizational audits, shifting organizational "context," and engineering organizational "breakdowns" in order to move beyond incrementalism.

1993   W. Warner Burke: *Organizational Development: A Process of Learning and Changing.* Excellent introduction.

1994   Wendell French et al.(eds): *Organizational Development and Transformation: Managing Effective Change.*

1995   William Rothwell (ed.): *Practicing Organization Development: A Guide for Consultants.*

2000   Jerry W. Gilley: *Organizational Learning, Performance, and Change: An Introduction to Strategic Human Resource Development.*

2001   Jay Shafritz and J. Ott (eds.): *Classics of Organization Theory.*

See also
Action Learning
Management Theory, People-Centered

Paradigm

Paradigm: a constellation of concepts, values, perceptions and practices shared by a community, which forms their vision of reality.
—Thomas Kuhn, 1962

A paradigm is a mindset or "mental model" (from the Greek). In ages past, in the world of philosphy, it has also been referred to as a world view or belief system or "spirit of the time"; in psychology it has been called an episteme (way of knowing) by the epistemologists and a schema by the phenomenologists.

Whatever version we invoke, a paradigm is generally a belief held by a group or organization. The belief is seldom stated explicitly and it is generally unquestioned. An example of a paradigm is the "training" paradigm, whose assumption is: "I am a trainer and whatever you bring to me to fix (like the proverbial man with the hammer), I will fix it by delivering a course to you. That is my job." A paradigm "shift," on the other hand, designates a fundamental *change in perspective*. For instance, if the paradigm shifts to a "performance" oriented perspective, you would say: "I am a performance consultant and will be happy to diagnose what's wrong; if it's a training problem our training department will be able to help you out; otherwise, if it's a compensation, motivation, managerial, or process problem, I will direct you to the right resource." The mental paradigm shift has caused you to change your stance from a focus on training activity to business results.

The concept of the paradigm shift was introduced and promoted by Thomas Kuhn (1922–1996) in his 1962 book, *The Structure of Scientific Revolutions*. The shift referred to here is the mind set that accompanies each major breakthrough epoch in science, as in the shift during the 1600s from Aristotle's static paradigm of descriptive science to Galileo's and Newton's dynamic view of a quantitative science. A later shift would occur around 1900 when Newton's own paradigm would be replaced by Einstein's paradigm of relativity.

Paradigms in Learning and Performance

The concept of the paradigm was first applied to the learning and performance arena in the early 1990s by Richard Pascale and several other key management theorists. Until we break our old mindsets, Pascale writes, new models of change, learning, and performance are not possible. Moreover, only when we see old problems in a new light does the real problem show up—and only then are we able to address it. Otherwise we're simply going about fixing old problems (like the trainer delivering training classes when training is not the answer). As Pascale sums up, we need to constantly "disturb equilibrium" in our organizations if we are to maintain the creative ability to bring appropriate solutions and change.

FASTPATHS

1931   Kurt Lewin: "The Conflict Between Aristotelian and Galileian Modes of Thought in Contemporary Psychology," *Journal of Genetic Psychology* 5 (1931): 141–177. Stresses that modern psychology should make the paradigm shift from thinking in static Aristotelian terms to the dynamic terms of Galileo. Extremely influential paper in psychology.

1957   Thomas Kuhn: *The Copernican Revolution.* On the paradigm shift from an earth-centered view of the universe to a sun-centered one.

1959   Fred E. Emery: *The Emergence of a New Paradigm of Work.*

1962   Thomas Kuhn: *The Structure of Scientific Revolutions.*

1985   Joel Barker: *Discovering the Future: The Business of Paradigms.*

1990   Richard Pascale: *Managing on the Edge: How the Smartest Companies Use Conflict to Stay Ahead.* Lucid and compelling on mindsets and mental maps as the hidden drivers in the world of learning and performance. Includes case studies. See in particular the chapter on "Disturbing Equilibrium."

1992   Joel Barker: *Future Edge: Discovering the New Paradigms of Success.*

▬ Performance Improvement and ▬ Performance Consulting

Performance Improvement: The Scientific Model

Expect performance from your promises.
—Shakespeare, Henry VI, 1591

Performance improvement is based on a classic scientific model, that of medicine and the medical intervention. The model provides a useful introduction to the four major steps involved in any performance improvement process.

1. *Diagnosis:* "Any changes in your weight recently?"
■ The differential gap analysis

2. *Prescription:* "Here's a prescription."
■ A solution or intervention based, not on the surface symptoms of the problem, but on the real root cause of the problem

3. *Administer Treatment:* "Take two aspirin before going to bed."
■ The implementation or deployment of the intervention or solution

4. *Checkup:* "Call me in the morning."
■ Follow-on continuous evaluation and assessment

The origins of modern performance improvement and performance consulting go back to the early 1900s and Frederick Taylor, who invented process-centered management consulting (see Fastpaths 1987, Weisbord). The methodology went through numerous incarnations, including the twists and turns of scientific and humanistic management consulting, to emerge in the management consulting arms of the Big Five accounting firms. The movement continued to gain ground in the late

---

Plato: "Socrates, what is performance improvement?"

Socrates: "Training and development—but with its eyes opened beyond the doors of the training room."

Plato: "And how do you practice it?"

Socrates: "The way I teach—by asking questions. There are four of them:

First, where do we want to be? This describes the future state of the organization.
Second, where are we now? This describes the current state.
Third, how do we get from here to there? Is it affordable and does it make good business sense?
Fourth, how will we know when we get there; how will we measure success?"

1990s when training departments and individual consultants started transforming themselves from tactically-oriented order takers into *business performance* consultants.

The theoretical basis for the movement came from a variety of sources, including classic works in behaviorism, cognitivism, and organizational development.

> In performance consulting as in medicine, prescription *before* diagnosis is malpractice.

The Four-Step Process Model of Performance Improvement and Consulting

Here is the expanded model of Performance Improvement and Consulting:

I. Diagnose the Problem: The Seven Performance Factors

Analyze the business problem, comparing current with optimum performance, and identify the cause from among the following seven factors:

1. *Expectations*: Are there clear job descriptions and performance expectations for employees?
2. *Consequences*: Are employees being paid for desired results, or for something else? Are rewards and recognitions, incentives and motivation directed toward the desired result?
3. *Support*: Do employees have the necessary support and resources to do their job?
4. *Feedback*: Are employees receiving feedback on how they're doing? Are they being praised when they do perform well?
5. *Processes*: Are processes and hand-offs between departments efficient? Are these processes aligned with organizational goals?
6. *Attitudes*: What is the attitude of management toward the business problem—and toward the potential solution? Attitudes form perceptions—which in turn shape reality—in corporations.
7. *Training*: Are people properly trained? Do they have the necessary knowledge, skills, and attitudes to do their job?

(Note: these seven factors are adapted from the works of Rummler, Skinner, Gilbert, and Mager.)

Scientific Method: An Ancient Craft

Just a few years ago, an ancient scroll called "The Surgical Papyrus" was unearthed in Egypt, which describes the steps necessary to carry out medical interventions. They are as follows:

1. Examine the symptoms
2. Diagnose the cause of the problem
3. Treat the malfunction
4. Note any lessons learned

The papyrus states that this same process is followed, whether one is treating "a fracture, a dislocation, or a sprain." Date of the original papyrus? Probably 3000 B.C.—5,000 years ago! Process interventions are a very ancient craft.

—Adapted from Frederick Kilgour,
The Evolution of the Book, 1998

II. Prescribe a Solution

Select a solution or intervention that is aligned with the business goals of the company. Create clear, measurable objectives for the solution. The more specific the solution and measure of success, the better chance it has of succeeding.

III. Administer the Treatment

Architect the solution. If training, build the course or the job aid, or set up the coaching procedures, etc. If not training, revise the salary structure, improve hiring procedures, or create a new business unit.

IV. Check Up on the Results

This is the all-important, final step, which ensures the accountability of the project and its contribution to the economic health of the organization. It consists of periodic "performance checks" throughout the organization to validate that improvement is indeed occurring. If not, the transfer of training (Level 3 evaluation) processes should be revisited.

Summary: Improving Business Effectiveness

Performance improvement and consulting is high-level organizational troubleshooting, its aim being to effect measurable behavior change in an organization. It systematically diagnoses what's wrong with an organization, prescribes a solution, and carries out the implementation of that solution, to the ultimate end of improving bottom-line financial results. Its watchwords are organizational efficiency and effectiveness.

The concept of performance improvement is so broad-based that the literature on it is endless. The following Fastpaths section presents a mere sampling of the available literature.

FASTPATHS

1987   Marvin Weisbord: *Productive Workplaces.* Weisbord, in a highly readable history of organizational development, touches on many aspects of performance improvement, covering theory as well as practice.

1990   Geary Rummler (with Alan Brache): *Improving Performance: How to Manage the White Space on the Organization Chart.* Superb study on methods of performance improvement and consulting. Highly recommended as one of the best books ever written on this topic. Rummler is a master.

1992   H. Stolovitch and E. Keeps (eds.): *Handbook of Human Performance Technology.* An 800-page volume by various hands; for professionals.

"Performance": A Loaded Word

When I hear the word "performance," to paraphrase a famous writer, I reach for my revolver. The word is loaded in every sense. Lifted from the worlds of sport and high finance, the word carries connotations of precision, power, and high impact. Think for a minute about the following examples:

Sports: Professional athletes' *performance* is measured in triple-doubles (basketball), sacks-per-game (football), and runs batted in (baseball). A Formula One race car hits peak *performance* at 15,000 RPMs.

Finance: Corporate *performance* is measured by P/E ratios, investment portfolios by ROI, and stock market *performance* by numbers on the Dow and the Nasdaq.

With its heritage of precision and continuous monitoring anchored in numbers, *performance* provides us a lot to live up to in the world of performance improvement.

—David H. Miles

1994   John Noonan: *Elevators: How to Move Training Up from the Basement.* Good introduction for beginners moving training "up" to performance and ROI considerations.

1994   Richard Swanson: *Analysis for Improving Performance: Tools for Diagnosing Organizations and Documenting Workplace Expertise.*

1995   James and Dana Robinson: *Performance Consulting: Moving Beyond Training.* Good introduction to the field.

1996   Dana and J. Robinson: *Performance Consulting.* A solid introduction to the field.

1997   David Ripley and Peter Dean: *Performance Improvement Pathfinders: Models for Organizational Learning.* History of a dozen pioneers in the field.

1997   Robert Mager and P. Pipe: *Analyzing Performance Problems.* The classic text on analyzing performance problems, recently updated.

1998   Allison Rossett: *First Things Fast: A Handbook for Performance Analysis.* Quick read, clear introduction.

1998   Judith Hale: *The Performance Consultant's Fieldbook.* Basic work by an expert in the field of performance evaluation.

2000   Danny Langdon: *Aligning Performance.* Solid book on aligning performance across an organization.

2002   Harold Stolovitch and E. Keeps: *Telling Ain't Training.* A book on how and why we learn, and how to make learning stick.

See also
Behaviorism
Cognitivism
Human Performance Technology

Reengineering

The best strategy is not one that tries to divine the future, but one that creates the ability to respond rapidly to the present.
—Michael Hammer, 1993

In 1993, fast on the heels of Deming's TQM movement of the 1980s, Michael Hammer published *Reengineering the Corporation: A Manifesto* and launched the systems reengineering movement of the 1990s. Reengineering, in Hammer's words, is "the fundamental rethinking and radical redesign of business processes to bring about dramatic improvements in performance." The five main objectives of reengineering are:

1. Boost growth
2. Build market share
3. Improve competitive stance
4. Improve financial results
5. Promote teamwork

Reengineering's Vision

The twenty-first century company, according to Hammer, will be organized around processes rather than functions. Managers will coach and design rather than supervise and control. Employees will be processor-performers rather than task-workers, and they will have a broad understanding of their company. The company itself will be a dynamic, flexible organization, filled with entrepreneurial zeal and focused sharply on customer needs, an organization where every employee is important. People will be treated as assets and not as expenses.

The organization of the future will no longer cling to traditional hierarchical structures and bureaucratic systems. The future will belong to the processed-centered organization, in which self-directed performers will be focused on creating customer value rather than performing as mere industrial-era drones. "We have institutionalized the ad hoc and enshrined the temporary," states Hammer, suggesting that corporate hierarchies should be eliminated, and replaced with streamlined "process" teams made up of marketing, manufacturing, sales, and service personnel that use computers to combine tasks and therefore can work with less supervision.

Hammer states that the real point of reengineering is not getting rid of people but "getting more out of people, targeting strategic long-term growth on the revenue side." However, the all-out techno-fervor of reengineering tends to overlook the "people factor" in performance, as well as the downsizings that impair performance as much as improve it. Still, much of reengineering, when applied in a people-centered performance system, remains absolutely valid.

See also
Total Quality Management

FASTPATHS

1990   Michael Hammer: "Reengineering Work: Don't Automate, Obliterate" *Harvard Business Review* (August 1990).

1993   Michael Hammer and J. Champy: *Reengineering the Corporation: A Manifesto for Business Revolution.*

1993   Richard Pascale and others: "The Reinvention Roller Coaster," *Harvard Business Review* (November–December 1993). Urges reengineering to move beyond incrementalism toward quantum reinvention of companies.

1995   Michael Hammer and S. Stanton: *The Reengineering Revolution: A Handbook.* Largely a follow-on work to the earlier *Reengineering* of 1993.

1996   Michael Hammer: *Beyond Reengineering: How the Process-Centered Organization Is Changing Our Work and Our Lives.* Hammer shifts from promoting pure reenginering to promoting the customer-driven organization. Very valuable insights.

1996   Joseph White: "Reengineering Gurus Take Steps to Remodel Their Stalling Vehicles: Mike Hammer and Others Broaden Their Offerings, Push Growth Strategies" (*Wall Street Journal,* November 26, 1996). Reengineering confesses its shortcomings, that it "forgot the people part of processes," and mends its ways.

2001   Michael Hammer: *The Agenda: What Every Business Must Do to Dominate the Decade.* Hammer continues his shift from a focus on pure systems to one promoting the customer-driven organization, advancing the notion of a web-based Enterprise System "open to the customer." Extremely useful ideas, as Hammer is a good systems thinker and an exceptionally clear writer.

Return on Investment and Cost-Benefit Analysis

ROI is profit or savings (benefit) divided by capital invested (cost).
                                            —David H. Miles

Return on investment (ROI), an accounting invention by DuPont during the 1920s, is increasingly being invoked in the world of learning and performance. Here are some initial definitions and steps, plus pointers to expert texts on the topic, and also an explanation of cost-benefit analysis, which is directly related.

ROI is a measure of financial performance that is used to project revenue or savings in order to position the cost of training as an "investment" rather than a cost. In its simplest terms, ROI is defined as return (or profit or earnings during a given accounting period) divided by the capital that was invested. Here is the formula:

$$\text{ROI} = \frac{\text{Return}}{\text{Investment}} = \frac{\text{Increase in Revenue or Savings} - \text{Cost}}{\text{Cost}}$$

To make this clearer, let's take an example. Let's assume that during your first year as training manager you spend $100 for training, and that this results in $125 of additional sales for that year. The formula would look like this:

$$\frac{\$125 \text{ increase in sales through training/yr} - \$100 \text{ spent for training/yr}}{\$100 \text{ spent for training/yr}}$$

$$= \frac{\$25 \text{ return/yr}}{\$100 \text{ investment/yr}} \quad \times \quad 100 \text{ (percent)} \quad = 25 \text{ percent ROI/year}$$

Note that one must always give the time period involved, in this case a year. *ROI is always for a specific period of time; otherwise it is meaningless.* This time period must be included in the final figure, as "an ROI of 25 percent per year." The challenge in calculating ROI for training is in attaching dollars and cents to what is often an abstraction, namely *improved performance.* The books listed in the Fastpaths section below will help you along this route.

Cost-Benefit (Inverse ROI)

ROI can be computed either *before* or *after* a training initiative. If afterwards, it assesses the payback or breakeven point in time of an investment; if computed beforehand, it represents a projected ROI, and this projection is sometimes called a *cost-benefit analysis.* Like ROI, cost-benefit analysis can be extremely complex, but is always used for the same basic purpose: to determine whether a given initiative is worth funding. It sets out the factors that need to be taken into consideration in making such an economic decision, and as such, it is an essential tool for strategic planning and decision-making. Cost-benefit analysis (projected ROI) asks the basic question: "Will this given project save more money in the long run than it costs?" Using the previous ROI example (a $100 cost and a $25 benefit or return), the cost-benefit ratio would be 4 to 1 (per year), as follows:

$$\frac{\text{Cost}}{\text{Benefit}} = \frac{\$100 \text{ (Investment)}}{\$25 \text{ (Return)}}$$

Notice that cost-benefit is the same thing as projected ROI, but with the numbers inverted: A 25-percent ROI, as in the present example, represents a 4-to-1 cost-benefit ratio.

FASTPATHS

1971   Ezra J. Mishan: *Cost-Benefit Analysis*. A classic text, updated numerous times since.

1972   Richard Layard (ed.): *Cost-Benefit Analysis: Selected Readings.* The Introduction and Part I provide good overviews. Updated several times since.

1983   Jack J. Phillips: *Handbook of Training Evaluation and Measurement Methods.* One of several titles by Phillips, who specializes in evaluation and ROI. Available in more recent editions as well.

1986   Lyle Spencer: *Calculating Human Resource Costs and Benefits: Cutting Costs and Improving Productivity.*

1995   John Noonan: *Elevators: How to Move Training Up from the Basement.* Noonan, basing his work on Lyle Spencer (1986), adds a creative suggestion for extrapolating Level 4 ROI from Level 1 interview data—when no financial data for ROI is available. Offbeat but plausible in certain situations, given appropriate disclaimers. (See "Tips for Level 4" in Evaluation: The Four Levels and ROI section.)

1996   Anthony Boardman et al. (eds.): *Cost-Benefit Analysis: Concepts and Practice.* Updated several times since.

1997   Jack Phillips: *Handbook of Training Evaluation and Measurement Methods.*

2000   Jac Fitz-enz: *The ROI of Human Capital.*

2001   Matthew Adler and E. Posner (eds.): *Cost-Benefit Analysis: Legal, Economic, and Philosophical Perspectives.*

2002   Patricia Phillips: *The Bottom Line on ROI: Basics, Benefits, and Barriers to Measuring Training and Performance Improvement.*

See also
Evaluation, Level 4

Strategic Planning

Strategic planning refers to the process by which an organization maps out its economic future, and the steps by which it will achieve its business purpose over time. This process typically considers four factors: internal Strengths and Weaknesses, and external Opportunities and Threats (SWOT being the common acronym). It also identifies the goals, functions, priorities, and resources that will be necessary to achieve its purpose. Over the last half century there have been at least six major swings or phases in strategic planning (see Fastpaths 1995, Koch) and the paradigm march continues. Where training tends to function at the managerial level and organizational development at the executive level, strategic planning tends to occur at the boardroom level.

FASTPATHS

1962 Alfred Chandler: *Strategy and Structure.* One of the first major books in the field, defined strategy as setting long-term goals and objectives, determining a course of action, and allocating resources to achieve those goals.

1980 Michael Porter: *Competitive Strategy: Techniques for Analyzing Industries and Competitors.* Porter remains an academic phenomenon to this day, but is difficult to access for the uninitiated.

1982 Kenichi Ohmae: *The Mind of the Strategies: The Art of Japanese Business.* Still one of the best explanations of how strategy plays out in the real world.

1988 John Bryson: *Strategic Planning for Public and Nonprofit Organizations: A Guide to Strengthening and Sustaining Organizational Achievement.*

1994 Gary Hamel and C. K. Prahalad: *Competing for the Future.*

1994 Henry Mintzberg: *The Rise and Fall of Strategic Planning: Reconceiving Roles for Planning, Plans, Planners.*

1995 Marvin Weisbord: *Future Search: An Action Guide to Finding Common Ground in Organizations and Communities.*

1995 Richard Koch: *The Financial Times Guide to Strategy: How to Create and Deliver a Useful Strategy.* A superb book for the beginner as well as intermediate practitioner. Koch, with great lucidity, explains not only the theory but also the practice, including a do-it-yourself guide in Part I. Concludes with an A to Z of strategic thinkers, tools and techniques, and concepts and definitions. A great book to start with.

1997 Sumantra Ghoshal and Christopher Bartlett: *The Individualized Organization.* Stresses people, processes, and purpose.

2002 Tony Manning: *Making Sense of Strategy*. Manning addresses the philosophy, products, positioning, and partners that go into strategic planning. A clear, brief exposition of the topic.

See also
Organizational Development

Total Quality Management

Quality control must be built into the front end of the manufacturing cycle, not viewed as a last-minute check to be done just before goods are shipped.

—Don Marchand and Forest Horton: *Infotrends* (1986)

Total Quality Management (TQM) is a data-driven continuous improvement methodology that places great emphasis on product quality and customer satisfaction. Typically led by senior management and driven by organization-wide teams, TQM got its start in the 1980s with the work of W. Edwards Deming, who had used the technique with enormous success in Japan (see Deming). TQM was the unspoken force behind Michael Hammer's "reengineering" (process redesign) of the 1990s and lies behind today's customer-focused "continuous performance improvement" movements as well.

FASTPATHS

1924 Walter Shewhart, a statistician at Bell Labs and grandfather of Total Quality Management (TQM), develops the Statistical Process Control method (SPC). The SPC "control chart" uses statistical techniques to control unwanted variations on an assembly line in a manufacturing environment. By constantly monitoring the work, the chart "controls" the process, maintaining one that is *statistically stable*. Shewhart also formulates the Shewhart Learning and Improvement cycle, which combines creative management techniques with statistical analyses in a "Plan-Do-Study-and-Act" (PDSA) cycle. W. Edwards Deming, one of Shewhart's students, would popularize these quality control methods as TQM in the 1980s—adding Deming's own variation, called the Plan-Do-Check-Act cycle (PDCA), which is still used in the automotive industry today.

1951   Joseph Juran's *Quality Control Handbook* appears. During the late 1940s and the 1950s, Juran and W. Edwards Deming introduce statistical quality control methods to Japanese manufacturers (the United States is not yet interested). Thirty years later, during the 1980s, U.S. corporations catch on and the movement becomes Total Quality Management (as opposed to Total Quantity Management). In the 1990s some of these techniques, coupled with process reengineering, become part of the "performance improvement" movement.

1982   W. Edwards Deming: *Out of the Crisis.* Deming launches the TQM (total quality management) movement in the 1980s, which in the 1990s is transformed by others into process reengineering and performance improvement. Deming's success in post-World War II Japan pitted quality management against the quantity management of typical American industrial-age management. It would take others and the amazing success of the Japanese "economic miracle" to convince Americans to undertake total quality management.

> "If I can measure it, I can improve it."
> —Deming, *Out of the Crisis,* 1982

1991   Armand Feigenbaum: *Total Quality Control.* Feigenbaum notoriously emphasized that every employee and function in the organization was responsible for quality and customer satisfaction.

1994   Elaine Biech: *TQM for Training.* Excellent introduction to the field.

2001   S. Chowdhury: *The Power of Six Sigma.* The TQM quality improvement initiatives of the 1980s returned in the twenty-first century as "Six Sigma." Six Sigma is a statistical measure of quality control for assembly lines, designating less than 3.4 defects per one million units (sigma designates the estimated standard deviation).

See also
Deming

Zoom Design

Zoom design is an instructional systems design technique consisting of:

1. Displaying a big-picture view of what is to be learned, akin to the "establishing shot" of a house in the opening of a film

2. Zooming in to a sequence of detailed close-ups to explain the content in detail, in separate lessons

Good design also periodically "zooms out" for a big-picture view of where the learning-of-the-moment fits into the larger plan and sequence—for an integrated vision of the whole.

III. TEN LEARNING MASTERS

. . . gladly would he learn,
and gladly teach.

—Geoffrey Chaucer, *The Canterbury Tales,* A.D. 1390

Moses

The Ten Commandments of Learning Design and Delivery

And in the midst of the fire the Lord wrote ten commandments upon two tablets of stone and commanded Moses: "Teach."

—Deuteronomy 4 (800 B.C.)

The earliest learning that was designed before it was delivered occurred in the West with Moses and the Ten Commandments, and in the East with Confucius' *Great Learning*. In the West, the Old Testament is the first great document on written learning design and knowledge transfer, be it for an individual, a small group, or an organization.

These learning principles still hold true today, most obviously in training that requires the memorization of high-level strategic points, axioms, precepts, or first principles. If one is to transmit a new mission statement to an organization, for instance, this type of learning would be in order. Although no longer our sole method of knowledge transfer, memorization is still a vital *component* in any learning system. Using the Ten Commandments as examples, here are ten meta-commandments on how to design and deliver training.

The Ten Commandments of Learning Design and Delivery

I. Learning Design

1. Be Clear

   Compose your points as bullets and keep them simple.
   Example: "Honor thy father and mother."

2. Be Brief

   Do not overwhelm with too many bullets, for the people are a forgetful and distracted lot. Number the commandments 1 to 10, for instance, so the people can count them on their fingers, after they've gone home (as a job aid).
   Example: "Here are the ten statutes that I speak in your hearing today *so that you may learn them.*"

3. Define Key Terms and Give Examples
   Example: "A graven image is a carving, as in the carving of the likeness of a winged bird."

4. Sequence Points from Most Important to Least Important
   Open your sequence with the most important point: "Thou shalt have no other gods."
   Close with the least important: "Thou shalt not covet thy neighbor's donkey."

5. Dramatize Points: Capture Attention
   Utilize story-based metaphors, embedding axioms and precepts in vivid scenarios.
   Example: Inform students that your axioms appeared in the night on a distant mountaintop, which was "wrapped in thick darkness, clouds, and gloom, and is burning with fire."

II. Learning Delivery

6. Leverage Emerging Technology
   The Ten Commandments deploy the latest technology—the invention of writing. Writing was so new in fact that God himself had to design the first prototype, before carrying out the knowledge transfer (train the trainer) to Moses. Moses then carried the two stone tablets to the people and read them out loud, for the people could not yet read the new technology.

7. Use Train-the-Trainer Sessions
   The Lord delivers no fewer than eight train-the-trainer sessions on Mount Sinai to ensure that Moses will deliver the ten lessons correctly to his people.

8. Build Blended Solutions
   God tells Moses to deliver the commandments both instructor-led and through the technology of writing:

   ■ "Thou shalt talk of them."
   ■ "Thou shalt write them."

   Don't forget the power of a blended solution.

9. Make it Portable: Remember the Mobile User (the Roving Nomad)
   The Lord instructs Moses to write the commandments on two stones, so that they are portable, and also to construct a wooden box (ark) to carry them in so that they can be transported from

camp to camp. During their forty years in the desert, the nomadic users will thus have immediate access to the learning database.

10. Anytime, Anywhere Learning: In the Palm of Your Hand

"Thou shalt write the ten commandments upon the door posts of thy house, upon every gate, on the headband between thy eyes and yea, even in the palm of thy hand."

Follow-on performance support is crucial to any learning initiative.

Now get thee hence and beget much learning, for bad design and ineffectual delivery is a weariness unto the flesh!

FASTPATHS

The Old Testament: Exodus and Deuteronomy chapters

Socrates

Guided Discovery Learning

You have something within you, Theaetetus, that you're bringing forth.
—Socrates, 425 B.C.

The Kingdom of Knowledge Is Within: Early Constructivism

In contrast to Moses, who trekked across the vast deserts of the Near East carrying two giant stone Tablets of Learning, Socrates, 400 years later, traveled light. Sounding more like a Zen Buddhist or early Gnostic Christian, he held that the kingdom of knowledge was nowhere but within. The question, he added, was only how to call forth this knowledge from the learner. The learner, he pointed out, simply needed to be "awakened" to knowledge.

What is of interest to learning designers today is not the content of Socrates (the abstractions of mathematics), but the sophisticated method that he created: the dialogical model of learning that came to be known as the Socratic method. Twenty-five centuries later, transmitted by learning theorists such as Comenius and Herbart, the method has become the basis for modern constructivism and, in part, adult education—the theory that learners learn best when they reconstruct the truth through their own hands-on experience. The method works as follows.

Guided Discovery Learning: The Socratic Method

I don't "teach," I just ask questions.
　　　　　　　　—Socrates on the Socratic method, in Plato's *Meno*, 400 B.C.

From my teacher Parmenides I learned the teaching method of "question and answer," rather than delivering long lectures.
　　　　　　　　　　　　　—Socrates, in Plato's *Sophist*, 400 B.C.

The process through which Socrates elicits learning from his students is called dialectical or conversational learning and is best described as a form of guided or prompted discovery learning. The student undergoes an open-ended question-and-answer process, with the teacher functioning as a coach or prompter. Socrates demonstrates the method by guiding a new student through the elementary rules of geometry.

Instead of having the boy memorize abstract mathematical definitions, such as "a box is a square with four equal sides" (which would remain a meaningless abstraction), Socrates asks a question *while pointing* to the drawing of a real square: "Tell me, boy, did you know that a figure like this is called a square?" The boy answers "I do," and Socrates then calls forth the next concept: the definition that the area of a square equals the length of one side multiplied times itself. This is done again through direct observation rather than through memorization. Socrates draws a square on the ground, divides its interior into four boxes, and permits the student himself to count the squares in the area:

> If one side is two feet long and the other side is also two feet long, what is the area of the square? Isn't it two feet times two feet? How much is twice two feet? *Count the squares and tell me,* he tells the boy.

The boy counts the squares himself, and answers correctly, "four, Socrates"—and on it goes. At each step of the learning process there are embedded prompts by the teacher, each of them eliciting the next learning point. It should be emphasized that Socratic dialogue is not free-form dialogue, as is sometimes presumed. It is guided learning or prompted experiential learning, a method that still remains one of our most powerful learning tools, particularly for adult education.

FASTPATHS

400 B.C. Plato: *Meno.*

1892   Thomas Davidson: *Aristotle and Ancient Educational Ideals.*

1945   Robert Ulich: *History of Educational Thought.*

Plato

A Continuous Learning Organization

Plato's Republic *is the most beautiful educational treatise ever written.*

—Rousseau, 1762

Plato is the visionary among Greek learning theorists. If Socrates is the Great Conversationalist and Aristotle the Great Systems Thinker, Plato is the Theorist of the Learning Organization. Not only did he devise the first blueprint for a learning organization, but he also contributed the first theory of the psychology of learning. We will look first at his vision of the learning organization.

Design for a Continuous Learning Organization

And the teachers will continue learning as well.

—Plato, 400 B.C.

Plato outlines his vision for a continuous learning organization in the *Republic* and in the *Laws.* At the center of his system is the concept of the Philosopher King, a sort of CEO and Chief Learning Officer combined into one, which Plato terms a Director of Education. In the ideal Republic, learning is available to all:

> Schooling will be open to all and schools should be located in the city as well as the country. The Director of Education shall act as

general tutor and interpreter of material that is to be learned. Moreover he will direct the teachers to teach as well as to continue to
update their curricula. And he shall also insist that *the teachers
themselves shall continue learning as well.*

Plato's grand vision of a city-wide learning organization failed, but he
did manage to create a smaller version in Athens, which he called the
Academy. This school attracted such renowned students as Aristotle, who
in turn taught Alexander the Great. And with this academy, the tradition
of continuous learning, at least on a small scale, was initiated in the West,
and it would never be halted again.

The Psychology of Learning: The Three Domains

Two horses draw my chariot, Reason and Emotion.
—Parmenides, 450 B.C., Socrates' teacher

Drawing on theories of philosophers who came before, Plato initiated
the field of psychology, formulating three domains that, 2,500 years
later, remain practically unchanged in the hands of present-day learning
psychologists. Each of us, Plato writes, operates in three psychological
domains:

- We learn with one part of our nature
- We feel angry with another part
- And the third part is physical desire

In more modern terms the domains can be summarized as follows:

- Learning belongs to the knowledge domain
- Emotions belong to the feeling domain
- Desire belongs to the physical domain

These three domains, with a shift in the third domain to physical
skills, are the direct forerunners of our modern domains of "knowledge,
skills, and attitudes (emotions)" in the training arena (see following section on Aristotle).

Maxims from Plato

■ *The Charioteer "Reason" Steers Physical Skill and Emotional Attitude.* Reason, for Plato, is the defining trait in the learning process. Reason not only links knowing with doing but, in a famous analogy, he compares Reason to a charioteer steering two horses—the horses of Physical Skill and Emotional Attitude. Reason, according to Plato, keeps these in check and on track.

■ *Learning Through Games and Simulations.* Games and pleasure are prime motivators of learning, according to Plato. "Mathematics should be learned through recreational games, the way the Egyptians do, through amusement and pleasure."

■ *Learning Through the Theater of Humor.* Plato often portrayed learning as a form of theater: "Serious things must be understood through humorous things," he writes. In learning it is effective "to utilize characters and scenes from the theater and the world of comedy."

■ *Learning in Frequent Brief Intervals.* "The young always do better when the learning process is divided into brief but frequent intervals."

■ *A Blueprint for Lifelong Learning.* In laying down the rules for lifelong learning, Plato compares the process to the building of a ship of life: "Let us now speak of teaching," he writes in *The Laws*, "as the shipwright first sketches the blueprint of a ship in outline, laying down the lines of the keel before beginning construction, so we lay down here the blueprint for the voyage through life."

FASTPATHS

400 B.C.   Plato: *Republic* and *Laws*.

1892   Thomas Davidson: *Aristotle and Ancient Educational Ideals*.

1945   Robert Ulich: *History of Educational Thought*.

1947   Robert Ulich (ed.): *Three Thousand Years of Educational Wisdom*.

1966   Wade Baskin (ed.): *Classics in Education*.

Aristotle
Systems Thinking and Psychology

Aristotle (384–322 B.C.), "master of those who knew," as later philosophers would call him, single-handedly laid the foundations for modern systems thinking—the practice of analyzing the world in terms of object assemblages united by an interaction of parts. He also invented the discipline of psychology, and continued the lifelong learning mission of Socrates and Plato.

Systems Design: Aristotle and the Art of Chunking

First, divide the sciences into the theoretical and the applied. Then see if you can find a joint or parting in each of these subclasses, and so on.
—Plato, *Statesman*, 400 B.C.

True to his fascination with systems and classifying, Aristotle's life and works were a constant quest to collect, categorize, and catalogue knowledge. Characteristically, he owned the first private library (of scrolls), and he turned systems thinking into a fine art. (For a description of his ideas of decomposition, chunking, and hierarchical classification, see the section "Content Design: Chunking and Sequencing.")

Psychology: The Three Domains

"The psyche," Aristotle writes, "is characterized by three basic functions:

- Knowing
- Feeling
- Will-to-Action"

Astonishingly, this triadic structure of consciousness would hold sway right down to the present day, a period of more than 2,300 years. In the 1950s, behaviorists such as Benjamin Bloom would take this tripartite structure of consciousness and transform it into a taxonomy of training, with its three domains of knowing, feeling, and doing. From Plato to Aristotle, the structure looks like this:

Plato	*Aristotle*
Knowledge (learning)	Knowledge
Feeling (emotions)	Feeling
Desires (physical)	Will-to-Do (physical)

From Aristotle to Bloom, it looks like this:

Aristotle	*Bloom*
Knowledge (head)	Knowledge (cognitive realm, thinking)
Feeling (heart)	Attitude (emotional realm, feeling)
Will-to-Do (hands)	Skills (physical realm, doing)

Aristotle on Lifelong Learning

Aristotle, apart from inventing systems thinking and psychology, was also a firm believer in lifelong learning. Like Socrates and Plato before him, he insists that "the activity of learning occupies a lifetime," for "all men by nature desire to know."

FASTPATHS

350 B.C.   Aristotle: *On Psychology* ("On the Soul") and *On Memory.*
1892   Thomas Davidson: *Aristotle and Ancient Educational Ideals.*
1945   Robert Ulich: *History of Educational Thought.*
1966   Wade Baskin (ed.): *Classics in Education.*

Dante

Curriculum as Memory Theatre

When one thinks of the drawers in a Memory Theatre, they begin to look like one vast filing system.
                                   —Frances Yates, *The Art of Memory,* 1966

Dante's *Divine Comedy* (A.D. 1300), with its fantastic hells, vast purgatories, and backlit heavens, is, in a very real sense, a precursor of the World Wide Web. In fact Dante, as Frances Yates has pointed out, architected one of the most spectacular knowledge bases that the medieval world had ever seen. In her brilliant study, *The Art of Memory,* Yates describes Dante's creation as a virtual world or memory theater. Memory theaters, Yates explains, were those early mental database systems that ancient classical orators invented in order to aid them in memorizing long speeches. By visualizing key points as small rooms inside a "theater," orators could memorize enormous amounts of material for presentation. Lodged like "learning objects" in their heads, information and phrases could be retrieved on a random access basis.

Dante's poem, through its structure and iconic imagery, functioned in a similar way—much like a curriculum housing a database filled with information on medieval history, politics, literature, and theology. Each point was "chunked" and visualized with an icon, using three major design strategies, all three of which are still at the heart of information design today: architecture, iconic tagging, and (by subsequent scholars) indexing.

Architecting a Data Space: The Information Terrace

Dante actually designed his narrative as a series of landscapes: a vast nine-level pit (learning about hell), a nine-story mountain (learning about purgatory), and nine ascending concentric spheres in the sky (learning about heaven). Each of these twenty-seven hierarchical information spaces is then subdivided into circular stair steps or "terraces" so that the reader can more easily recall the individual learning points in the didactic narrative.

Tagging a Knowledge Object: The Mnemonic Icon

Dante's real brilliance comes into play, however, with his iconic visualization of the individual learning points. In each case he uses a vivid visual image (icon) for a concept, so that it could be retrieved in the individual memory more easily. On the Mountain of Purgatory, for example, he embeds the moral point that "envy is sinful." Instead of leaving the point as an abstract commandment ("thou shalt not be envious"), he describes a dramatic scene on that particular information terrace (database cell), in which the characters have their eyes glued permanently shut, so that they can't be envious any more. This vividly grotesque image is one the reader will undoubtedly long remember, and be able to retrieve in their personal memory bank. Where concept is wedded to visual image, no long sermons and explanations are necessary.

Indexing the Content: Search Engines for Dante's Curriculum

Soon after *The Divine Comedy* appeared, scholars set about indexing and footnoting the work (by canto and verse), in order to make its contents more accessible to medieval and renaissance learners. Explanatory links were added, for instance, to points on Florentine geography, Italian history, church politics, and Catholic theology. The work became, in effect, one of the first real knowledge bases in existence before the age of printing.

FASTPATHS

1300   Dante Alighieri: *The Divine Comedy.*
1966   Frances Yates: *The Art of Memory.*

Comenius

Learner-Centered Design

A seventeenth-century anticipation of programmed learning has also been found in the work of Comenius, who advocated teaching in small steps, no step being too great for the student who was about to take it. Programming is sometimes described simply as breaking material into a large number of small pieces, arranged in a plausible order.

—B. F. Skinner, 1964

Johannes Comenius (1592–1670) was a Renaissance man in every sense of the word. Born in what is present-day Czechoslovakia at the time of Shakespeare and Elizabethan England, he was one of the greatest visionaries and scientists of learning systems that the field of instruction has ever seen. Like so many scholars of the Renaissance, Comenius was by profession a Protestant churchman, yet on his own he represented a one-man revolution in the world of Renaissance learning.

Influenced by Bacon's scientific method and the major Renaissance theories of learning, Comenius exercised a lasting influence on such modern theorists as Dewey, Skinner, and Jean Piaget (the French developmental psychologist and founder of cognitive constructivist learning). Many of his ideas still wait to be utilized by twenty-first century systems-based designers.

The seven key points of Comenius's vision in summary form are:

1. *Doing* (actio): We learn by doing: This same cry will echo down the centuries through the voices of Rousseau, Pestalozzi, Dewey, and others.

2. *Learner-Centered* (autopraxis or self-paced exercises): We learn through self-paced exercises, reconstructing the truth individually and by ourselves. As in modern constructivist learning, learning should be learner-centric, not instructor-centric.

3. *Context-Situated* (contextus): We learn through context. In language learning, for instance, we should learn through conversational methods rather than through mindless rote learning.

4. *Systems Learning* (didactica magna or great learning system): We learn best when we learn through a systems approach. This is Comenius's key learning principle.

5. *Experience* (experientia): Education should relate to everyday experience, and learning should be through the senses rather than through abstractions.

6. *Multi-Media* (media pictus or visual media): We learn best when we learn through multiple media. Comenius was creator and advocate of the world's first multimedia textbook for teaching (featuring woodcut illustrations for learners). The textbook remained a force in education throughout Europe for 150 years.

7. *Global Knowledge* (pansophia or all-knowledge): Underlying all learning and learning systems, Comenius states, is the vision of a global knowledgebase, or "universal library." Comenius's prophecy would begin to be realized in the 1700s during the Enlightenment, with its production of learned encyclopedias.

Of Comenius's many works, the most important for our purposes are:

■ *The Gate of Languages Unlocked* (on learning foreign language).
■ *The Visible World* (an illustrated textbook for children).
■ *The Great Didactic* (a comprehensive theory of global education). Now regarded as a classic work on learning theory. As Piaget has pointed out, Comenius was the first learning theorist to conceive of a genuine "science" of education and learning.

The maxims that follow are taken from Comenius's *The Great Didactic*.

Maxims from Comenius

■ *We Learn by Doing.* "It is by working that we learn how to work, just as we learn how to act by acting."

■ *Constructivism: We Learn by Reconstructing the Lesson Ourselves.* "Students shall themselves seek, discover, discuss, do, and repeat by their own efforts, examine everything themselves without abdicating to the teacher's authority. The teacher should be left with the task of seeing that the task is completed."

■ *From Instructivist (Instructor-Centered) to Constructivist (Learner-Centered) Learning.* "To seek and to find a method of instruction by which *teachers may teach less, and learners may learn more.*"

■ *Use Multiple Media.* "Teach everything through the medium of the senses. Show learners pictures of the things that they must learn. The illustrations should be derived from the events of everyday life. For all knowledge begins with sensuous perception. By appealing to the ear, the eye, and the hands (real world applications) what is learned is thoroughly impressed on the eyes, the ears, the understanding, and the memory."

■ *Root Cause Analysis.* "It is impossible to find a remedy until we have discovered the real cause of the disease."

■ *Concrete Performance Goals and Objectives Are Necessary.* "State 'In so many years I will bring this student to such and such a point, and we are going to educate him in such and such a way.' This is necessary if the method of instruction is to be successful."

■ *Sequence the Content from Simple to Complex (Elaboration Theory).* "Proceed from what is easy to what is more difficult. The subject matter should be so arranged that the learners first get to know that which lies nearest their mental vision, then that which lies moderately near, then that which is more remote, and lastly, that which is farthest off."

■ *Learner-Centered Design (Not Instructor-Centered).* "The more the teacher 'teaches,' the less the student learns."

■ *On Sense and Memory, Comprehension and Decisions.* "Learners should first exercise their senses; then the memory; then the comprehension; and finally their judgment."

■ *Learner Attitude and Motivation Are Key.* "The desire to know should be excited in learners in every possible manner."

■ *Don't Forget Humor.* "The method of instruction should lighten the drudgery of learning: relieve explanations through a humorous or less serious tone."

■ *Case-Based Learning: Situated Cognition.* "Languages should not be learned from grammar, but from real-life authors."

■ *Three Rules of Systems Design.* "Unless goals are set, means provided to reach them, and a proper system devised for application of those means, it is easy for something to be omitted and for failure to step in."

■ *Avoid Jargon.* "All explanations should be given in a language that pupils understand."

■ *Toward a Science of Learning.* "To set forth a universal method of learning with such certainty that the desired result must of necessity follow. This is my goal."

FASTPATHS

1650   John Comenius: *The Great Didactic of John Amos Comenius* (translated by
       M. W. Keating, 1896).

1945   Robert Ulich: *History of Educational Thought.*

1957   Jean Piaget (ed.): *John Amos Comenius "Selections,"* selections from the
       writings of Comenius, the first great learning theorist of the western world, still
       relevant today.

▬▬▬ Rousseau ▬▬▬

Learning Through Experience

There should be a strong emphasis on learning by doing.
                                                    —U.S. Army, 1962

Experience is the name everyone gives to their mistakes.
                                                    —Oscar Wilde, 1900

Rousseau (1712–1778), a French thinker of profound originality, helped
move philosophy out of the abstractions of the Enlightenment into the
psychological realm of modern times. It is his theories that helped spark
"progressive education" in the United States in the 1920s and 1930s (via
Dewey), and the constructivist movement (via Piaget) in learning in the
1990s. As Dewey writes, "Rousseau's teaching that education is a process
of natural growth has influenced most theorizing about education since
his time" (*Schools of Tomorrow*, 1915). Rousseau's most important books
for his theory of learning are *The Social Contract, The Confessions,* and
Emile, the latter being an educational tract disguised as a novel. The following comments are taken from all three of these.

Maxims from Rousseau

■ *We Learn by Doing.* "True education consists less of precepts (lectures) than of practice."

■ *Learner-Centered Design.* "Begin by studying your learners."

■ *Learning Should Be Customized.* "Instruction must be individual."

■ *Learning Is Lifelong.* "Everything we do not have at our birth and which we need when we are grown is given us by education."

■ *Learn from the Territory, Not the Map.* "You think you're teaching him what the world is like; he's only learning the map."

■ *Sequence Learning from Simple to Complex (Mild to Strong).* *Example*: To accustom his pupil Emile to the sound of a gun, Rousseau starts with a small charge and proceeds to ever greater charges until Emile can tolerate the large explosion given off by a real gun. This "shaping" of a response became a cardinal tenet in twentieth-century behaviorism.

■ *Give Nature Time.* "Give nature time to work before you take upon yourself her business, lest you interfere with her dealings."

■ *Learning Should Be Self-Directed.* "Learners should always learn for their own ends and advantages, not for the ends of an abstract curriculum."

■ *Ignore Tradition: Innovate!* "I will not stop to prove the current education system is bad, countless others have done so before me."

■ *Don't Lose Sight of Powerful Theories from the Past.* "Plato's *Republic* is the most beautiful educational treatise ever written."

■ *Not Facts but a Methodology for Lifelong Learning.* "My object is not to furnish the mind with knowledge, but with a method of acquiring it whenever needed."

FASTPATHS

1762   Jean Jacques Rousseau: *Social Contract.*
1762   Jean Jacques Rousseau: *Emile.*
1781   Jean Jacques Rousseau: *The Confessions.*
1945   Robert Ulich: *History of Educational Thought.*

See also
Dewey
Constructivism

Herbart

A Spiral Model for Continuous Learning Design

Herbartian psychology has taught an ideal psychology for the school teacher.

—Dewey, 1899

Humanity educates itself continuously.

—Herbart, 1830

Johann Herbart (1776–1841), a German philosopher and psychologist, was a precursor of modern cognitive psychology as well as the father of the science of learning. He is particularly inspirational when it comes to content design.

Building on the insights of Aristotle and Kant before him, Herbart helped transform German Idealism into German Realism, thereby propelling education into the modern world. By translating the philosophical concepts of evolutionary systems into everyday realities, he came up with profoundly simple methods and models for designing content.

Although Herbart's writings are burdened with the difficult language of Germanic philosophy and do not surrender maxims easily, here is a sample of his vast range and the innovative directions of his thought.

Instructional Systems Design: A Spiral Model

Herbart's model shows there is an art to instruction.

—Dewey, 1899

Designing a course, states Herbart, consists in following a four-step process, which repeats itself over and over again in the process of reconfiguring material for a course. Each spiral of development proceeds through four steps (as it flows from simpler to more complex):

1. *Overview:* Presentation of new material
2. *Assimilation:* Comparison of material with what is already known

3. *Systematization:* Integration of old and new into a unified whole

4. *Application:* Application of new systematic insight to a concrete example

Following Step 4, the design process repeats itself, engaging the next learning point and addressing this with a new overview, and so forth.

Herbart was popular and influential in the United States in the early 1900s, thanks to advocacy by John Dewey and others, but then fell into obscurity. It is time now, in the twenty-first century, to revive him. His best insights into content design can improve our understanding of how we actually design courses.

Maxims from Herbart

■ *Learning's Foundation Is Psychology.* "There is only one correct method for education: its foundation is psychology."

■ *Information Is Not Learning.* "Mere information does not suffice."

■ *Learning Should Be Enjoyable.* "To be wearisome is the cardinal sin of instruction."

■ *Theory and Practice.* "In education, theory and practice go hand in hand."

■ *Sequencing and Linking Are Keys to Creative Design.* "Sequencing, arrangement, and coordination of what is to be learned—these create the real impact in the instructional process."

FASTPATHS

1832   Johann Friedrich Herbart: *The Application of Psychology to the Science of Education* (translated and edited by Beatrice Mulliner, 1898).

1916   John Dewey: *Democracy and Education.*

1945   Robert Ulich: *History of Educational Thought.*

1992   William Rothwell: *Mastering the Instructional Design Process* (section on "Content Analysis").

Dewey

Learning by Doing

Knowledge is the daughter of experience.
—Leonardo da Vinci, 1500

We believe only what we have experienced.
—Empedocles, early Greek philosopher, 450 B.C.

We learn by doing.
—John Dewey, *Schools of Tomorrow*, 1915

John Dewey (1860–1952), already a force in American education in 1900, exercised an increasing influence right down through the 1930s, particularly through his advocacy of the "progressive education" movement. His theories continue to live on today in Constructivism, with its learner-centered environment (see Constructivism). More popularizer than original theorist, Dewey very much mirrored his time, championing the trend away from Hegelian idealism toward experimental psychology and philosophical pragmatism, as exemplified in the works of William James. Dewey also caught the spirit of Darwinism and rode its evolutionary, organic thinking through a series of "ism's" variously termed experimentalism, instrumentalism, operationalism, and functionalism. Dewey's impact cut two ways. On the one hand he influenced progressive education, with its notoriously misguided emphasis on empty educational "method" at the expense of real content. But on the other hand, his writings promoted two aspects of educational theory and practice that are still central today:

- *Scientific Method:* Learning through observing
- *Empirical Experience:* Learning through doing

Dewey's two major books on learning were *How We Think* (1910), which recommends the use of the scientific method in educational psychology, and *Democracy and Education* (1916), which is a summary of the evolution of educational philosophies. The latter book takes the reader on a journey from the class-bound educational theories of Plato down through the individualistic theories of Rousseau and nation-state theories of Hegel, to the twentieth century's democratic theories of education. The excerpts below are taken from both these works.

Maxims from Dewey

■ *We Learn by Doing.* "Recognition of the natural course of development always starts with situations involving *learning by doing.*" "Education that associates *learning with doing* will replace the passive education of imparting the learning of others."

■ *We Learn by Observing, Reflecting, and Experimenting.* "The scientific interest which requires personal observation, reflection, and experimental activity will be added."

■ *Mastery Through Experience, Not Information.* "Master the problems of experience, not the piling up of information."

■ *Learning Is Continuous Learning.* "The educational process is its own end, one of continually reorganizing, reconstructing, transforming."

■ *Everyday Application Is Key.* "[Education carries an impact] as long as the student has a need for it and applies it to some situation of his own. Every new idea should be worked out in application."

■ *Learning Postulates Inquiring Minds.* "Schools are unfortunately better adapted, as John Stuart Mill said, to make disciples rather than inquirers."

■ *Practice, Not Theory.* "It is never as easy to fulfill requirements in practice as it is to lay them down in theory."

■ *Avoid Sheer Information Disconnected from Doing.* "Only in education—never in the life of farmer, sailor, merchant, physician, or laboratory experimenter—does knowledge mean primarily a store of information aloof from doing."

■ *Knowledge Comes from the Physical World (Practice and Reflection).* "Plato's 'knowledge' was based on cobblers, carpenters, and players of musical instruments."

FASTPATHS

1899   John Dewey: *Lectures in the Philosophy of Education.* Contains an interesting critique of Herbart, one of Dewey's forerunners. (See Herbart.)

1910   John Dewey: *How We Think.* See above for comments.

1915   John Dewey: *The School and Society.* Cites Pestalozzi, Froebel, and Montessori, among others, as his forerunners.

1915   John Dewey: *Schools of Tomorrow.* Along with the titles of 1910 and 1916, this is the third most important of Dewey's books on learning, and in many ways his most satisfying, thanks to the concrete examples involved. The book is a series of case studies of schools, with Rousseau's "natural development and growth" theme playing the lead role throughout the entire book. By "schools of tomorrow," Dewey is referring to "progressive" education, which will become the reigning educational creed for teachers in the 1920s and 1930s and later give rise to modern Constructivism, with its emphasis on Rousseauian "guided" experiential learning environments.

1916   John Dewey: *Democracy and Education.* See above for comments.

1945   Robert Ulich: *History of Educational Thought.*

1947   Robert Ulich: *Three Thousand Years of Educational Wisdom.*

1973   George Dykhuizen: *The Life and Mind of John Dewey.*

1981   Richard Bernstein: *John Dewey.*

1987   E. D. Hirsch: *Cultural Literacy.* Describes some of the damage that Dewey and the progressive education movement have done to American education through the privileging of educational "method" over content and knowledge; a sane plea for standards, competencies, and a back-to-basics movement.

1995   Alan Ryan: *John Dewey and the High Tide of American Liberalism.*

1996   Michael Sandel: "Dewey Rides Again," *New York Review of Books* (May 9, 1996).

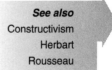

See also
Constructivism
Herbart
Rousseau

Deming

Total Continuous Learning

W. Edwards Deming (1900–1993) and his fourteen points are a mainstay in the performance improvement industry, particularly in the manufacturing sector. Although Deming is not a learning theorist, he is included here because of his enormous and lasting contribution to general process improvement and systems redesign. Deming's push after World War II for total "quality" management in manufacturing as opposed to total "quantity" management notoriously fell on deaf ears in the United States—but not in Japan, where it created an economic miracle.

It wasn't until the early 1980s, when Deming published his book *Out of the Crisis,* including the famous "Fourteen Points for Management," that American managers began to take note of his work. At this point TQM (total quality management) began to take off as a performance improvement movement. The fourteen points are still absolutely relevant for the twenty-first century and should reach the ears of people in learning and performance, as well as engineers interested in reducing cycle time and product errors on assembly lines.

Deming's Fourteen Points

Deming's famous fourteen points are summarized here, highlighting their application to learning and performance. Points relating directly to performance improvement are italicized. For the list of the original fourteen points, see Deming's *Out of the Crisis,* pp. 34–36.

1. A company's role is not to make money but to create a sense of purpose—a sense of purpose focused on the *constant improvement of its products and services.*
2. We are too tolerant of slipshod products and uninspired service.
3. Quality doesn't come from piecemeal inspection of products on an assembly line—but from improving the entire process itself.
4. Don't award business to vendors solely on price, but rather on quality—creativity, fit, features, benefits. Price is only one aspect

of the equation. *This is also true of learning and performance vendors and products.*

5. *Improve the system constantly and forever.* Improvement is not a one-time effort. We must improve it again and again.

6. *Implement proper training.* Workers generally can't do their jobs because no one ever trained them properly or was clear about what they should do. Implement proper training and performance improvement—both formal and on-the-job.

7. Supervisors shouldn't punish, but lead by example.

8. *Drive out fear of performance improvement:* The economic losses strictly from fear (people not daring to ask or to suggest improvements) are appalling.

9. Break down the barriers between staff areas—departments and units—to eliminate redundancy and to improve communication between processes.

10. *Eliminate slogans.* They never helped anybody really perform any better. Have employees come up with their own slogans and post these.

11. *Eliminate numerical quotas.* Replace them with quality-of-content measures.

12. *Remove barriers to pride of workmanship.* Most people are eager to do a good job. Performance improvement is sometimes nothing more than *the removal of the barriers to performance*—such barriers as fear of improving the system, unclear instructions, and misguided supervision (all above). Clarity in communication is all.

13. *Institute a vigorous program of education, self-improvement, and relearning.*

14. *Take action and accomplish the transformation.* Workers can't accomplish learning and performance improvements on their own; they require the sponsorship and follow-through of middle management.

FASTPATHS

1939   Walter Shewhart (with the editorial assistance of Deming): *Statistical Method from the Viewpoint of Quality Control.*

1950   W. Edwards Deming: *Some Theory of Sampling.*

1982   W. Edwards Deming: *Out of the Crisis: Quality, Productivity, and Competitive Position.*

1986   Mary Walton: *The Deming Management Method.*

1990   Mary Walton: *Deming Management at Work.*

1994   W. Edwards Deming: *Quotations of Dr. Deming: The Little Blue Book.*

See also
Reengineering
Total Quality Management

Index